The Anatomy of Psychotherapy

DATE DUE

The Anatomy
of Psychotherapy

Viewer's Guide to the APA Psychotherapy

Videotape Series

Gary R. VandenBos

Julia Frank-McNeil

John C. Norcross

Donald K. Freedheim

American Psychological Association

Washington, DC

First Printing June 1995
Second Printing November 2000

Published by the
American Psychological Association
750 First Street, NE
Washington, DC 20002

Copies may be ordered from
APA Order Department
P.O. Box 2710
Hyattsville, MD 20784

Typeset in Adobe Minion by Kachergis Book Design, Pittsboro, NC

Printer: Kirby Lithographic Company, Inc., Arlington, VA
Designer (cover and text): Kachergis Book Design, Pittsboro, NC
Technical/production editor: Valerie Montenegro
ISBN: 1-55798-335-6
ISBN: 1-55798-782-3

Printed in the United States of America

Contents

Introduction

The Videotape Series

The opening narration on each videotape concisely introduces the series in this way:

> The APA Psychotherapy Videotape Series presents distinguished psychotherapists of various orientations demonstrating their particular approach in entire, 40-minute sessions. Designed for clinical training and continuing education, the videotapes are spontaneous, unrehearsed sessions with professional actors. The actors portray clients based on actual case material. Although the sessions are unscripted, both the client and the therapist were conceptually and experientially anchored in the clinical material, each other, and previous sessions.

In the next few pages, we will build on this concise introduction by reviewing the development and purpose of the videotape series and by summarizing the objective and content of this viewer's guide.

Nowhere is the adage, A picture is worth a thousand words, truer than in demonstrating the practice of psychotherapy. Just as there is no better lesson in surgery than watching an operation in progress, there is no better lesson in psychotherapy than observing a session in progress. In this series, we have attempted to show the "anatomy of psychotherapy"—the sustained, detailed process of psychotherapists at work. The work is that of individual psychotherapy in an outpatient setting with adult clients; future tape series will demonstrate psychotherapy at work with children and adolescents and in different modalities.

The chosen psychotherapists represent a variety of theoretical systems and clinical styles. Our intent is to expose viewers to the breadth and depth of contemporary psychotherapy without value judgment, just as a professor would ideally teach the human anatomy. Neither the editors nor the American Psychological Association (APA) are endorsing any particular approach. We do hope, however, that the videotaped demonstrations and this *Viewer's Guide* will enhance the critical analysis of these psychotherapy systems. What are the strengths of this clinical approach? What might be some alternative ways of responding or interacting? What types of patients, disorders, and circumstances would be most suited to this form of psychotherapy? What empirical research supports the efficacy of this approach? We hope these and similar questions will be seriously considered in watching the APA Psychotherapy Videotape Series.

The goal of each videotape is to present an unrehearsed session that captures, to the fullest extent possible, the theoretical approach and clinical style of the particular psychotherapist. Toward this end, a number of steps were taken to ensure that both the therapist and the client were anchored, conceptually and experientially, in the clinical material, each other, and previous sessions. First, therapists identified the type of patient or clinical problem with which they typically work. Second, an actual client profile was developed by an independent team that included demographic data, presenting problem, precipitating event, clinical history, and other background information. Third, the therapists reviewed this profile for its representativeness and then described what would have transpired in the first two or three sessions. Fourth, professional actors adept in improvisation were immersed in this clinical history and patient presentation. Formal role induction was conducted by a clinical psychologist to affirm that the actor had both a cognitive understanding and an experiential sense of what the patient was struggling with, thinking, and feeling. Fifth and finally, the actor (in role) and the therapist interacted immediately prior to the videotaping, reviewing the case history and the process notes of their "earlier session," so that they were both anchored in the context of the therapy before the videotaping.

The end result is a spontaneous psychotherapy session, representing the third or fourth meeting in an ongoing course of psychotherapy and lasting 40 to 45 minutes in duration. This format is in marked contrast to other available tapes that provide snippets of dramatic re-creations of psychotherapy sessions. Although none of the distinguished psychotherapists would judge their sessions as their best work, they all agreed that the session was successful in demonstrating some aspects of their typical way of working with patients. The videotapes are useful, spontaneous illustrations in which one will find both strengths and weaknesses. Therapists benefit from good examples and bad examples alike in training. Like the human anatomy laid bare, the psychotherapists have purposefully, courageously exposed themselves and their methods for the purpose of education.

The APA Psychotherapy Videotape Series was designed for clinical training as well as continuing education. Among the anticipated uses are (a) learning how prominent practitioners carry out their sessions; (b) concretely illustrating theoretical concepts in psychotherapy; (c) gaining a firsthand look at what occurs in psychotherapy; (d) comparing the technical interventions and relationship stances associated with different systems of psychotherapy; (e) observing how therapists deal with particular critical incidents in treatment (e.g., dealing with patient anger toward the therapist); (f) training in specific therapeutic interventions (e.g., empty-chair technique); and (g) providing material for psychotherapy process research.

The *Viewer's Guide*

We, the editors of the Series, have prepared this *Guide* to assist you, the viewer, in using and learning from the videotapes. Specifically, we have prepared 12 chapters corresponding to the 12 videotapes in the series. The chapters are arranged in alphabetical order by the therapist's name. Each chapter follows the same format:

- **Autobiographical Sketch of the Psychotherapist**
  To acquaint you with the educational background, professional positions, and representative achievements of the clinician.
- **Synopsis of the Clinical Approach**
  To introduce you to the guiding framework and principal practices of this type of psychotherapy. This section can obviously offer only a brief introduction; the Suggested Readings provide references to more detailed expositions.

- **Client Background and Precipitating Events**
  To ground you in the relevant histories, recent experiences, and presenting problems of the patient portrayed in the videotape. This section contains all the information available to the psychotherapist prior to the taped session, so that you and the therapist occupy a level "playing field."
- **Process Notes From Initial Sessions**
  To familiarize you with the therapist's typical way of working with clients in the first two or three meetings preceding the videotaped session. This section includes information on rapport building, assessment methods, history taking, therapeutic contracting, early homework assignments, and any other goals or activities that the therapist would seek to accomplish prior to the third or fourth session.
- **Viewer's Notes**
  To provide you space to record your own reactions, questions, and comments while observing the demonstration session.
- **Stimulus Questions About the Videotaped Session**
  To prompt you to critically analyze therapeutic choice points in the videotaped session. We present questions about points in the therapy where some change in the focus or shift in the session occurs. These questions are not intended to criticize the actions of the therapists, but rather to stimulate active thinking and constructive dialogue about the practice of psychotherapy.
- **Therapist's Reflections on the Demonstration**
  To provide you with an edited transcription of the therapist's reflections on the videotaped session.
- **Suggested Readings**
  To direct you to more extensive written works on this form of psychotherapy. The videotaped psychotherapists recommended these sources, approximately half of which were authored by them, and approximately half of which pertain to the broader literature on the psychotherapy approach. When references were cited in the Synopsis, they were also included in the Suggested Readings.

We sincerely hope that the APA Psychotherapy Videotape Series enhances your appreciation of the complexity and the efficacy of the anatomy of psychotherapy.

CHAPTER 1

Feminist Therapy

Conducted by Laura S. Brown, PhD

About Dr. Brown

Laura S. Brown, PhD, received a bachelor's degree (1972) in psychology from Case Western Reserve University and a masters degree (1975) and doctorate (1977) in clinical psychology from Southern Illinois University at Carbondale. She is in independent practice as a psychotherapist and forensic psychologist in Seattle, WA and is clinical professor of psychology at the University of Washington. She has received the Distinguished Publication Award of the Association for Women in Psychology, the Leadership Citations of the American Psychological Association (APA) Committee on Women in Psychology and the APA Committee on Lesbian and Gay Concerns, and the Distinguished Psychologist Award of the Washington State Psychological Association. She holds the Diplomate in Clinical Psychology of the American Board of Professional Psychology and is a Fellow of the APA and the American Psychological Society. Dr. Brown is the author of numerous scholarly books and journal articles; her most recent book is *Subversive Dialogues: Theory of Feminist Therapy* (1994).

What do you know about Dr. Brown? What are your impressions of her work from published material, conversations with and about her, or any other sources of information?

What are your expectations of Dr. Brown's style and behavior in conducting psychotherapy?

Synopsis of Feminist Therapy
Provided by Laura S. Brown, PhD

Feminist psychotherapy is a technically eclectic approach to treatment, based conceptually and philosophically in feminist political analysis and feminist scholarship on the psychology of women and gender. Unique among approaches to psychotherapy, feminist therapy grounds itself within the context of a movement for justice and social change and has its roots in the critiques of dominant culture that have been raised by the second wave of the American women's movement. Consequently, feminist therapists perceive their work as one aspect of an overall feminist movement, and the process of therapy as one means for achieving social transformation at the personal level. Feminist therapy concerns itself not only with individual suffering but also with the social and political meanings of both pain and healing. Although superficially the work of a feminist therapist may appear to differ little from that of other practitioners, the manner in which this context-oriented philosophy of treatment gives meaning to what is occuring in the therapy session leads to some important differences between feminist and other approaches to psychotherapy.

Feminist therapy first emerged in the late 1960s when a number of feminists both within and outside the mental health disciplines began to develop critiques of how then-extant practices colluded with societal oppression of women. Chief among these critiques was Phyllis Chesler's groundbreaking work, *Women and Madness* (1972). Chesler was among the first psychologists to analyze the similarities between the therapist–client relationship as it was then commonly constructed—male, authoritative therapist and female patient—and the structure of social relationships between women and men in a sexist society. She began the process of identifying the ways in which therapy was harmful to women because it failed to address or remediate, and often perpetuated, the ways in which women were the targets of bias, discrimination, and violence. Other writers identified the stereotyped beliefs about women that lay at the core of then-dominant perspectives on personality, psychopathology, and psychotherapy. Naomi Weisstein, a physiological psychologist and feminist activist, called attention to the manner in which women's behavior was assumed to be biologically based and instinctual, drawing upon flawed and biased animal research that was then inappropriately generalized to women. She noted the manner in which certain psychoanalytic hypotheses about women's personality—particularly women's masochism, passivity, and dependency—had become reified as norms for female functioning (Weisstein, 1970). Inge Broverman and her colleagues demonstrated empirically that these beliefs were held by experienced mental health professionals when their research participants defined mentally healthy adult women as more passive, dependent, and unable to function in a crisis than either mentally healthy men or mentally healthy adults (without gender specified).

Feminist therapy is also unique among approaches to psychotherapy in that it has no founding leader or teacher. Instead, it has been developed by a multitude of feminist practitioners across the mental health disciplines, working from the grass roots to develop a convergence of opinion regarding what constitutes feminist practice. Epistemologically bound to the data of clinical experience, feminist therapy theory reflects the deliberations and discussions of 25 years of work by therapists attempting to apply feminist analysis to the variety of problems faced by mental health practitioners.

Although initially the efforts of feminist therapy were directed toward treatment of women clients—to the degree that any treatment of women has at times been mistaken for feminist therapy—the past decade has seen an expansion of feminist analysis to a broader range of patient populations and practice arenas. This extension has led to a greater understanding of the importance of feminist theory and analysis, as differentiated from that of the gender of either client or therapist, to feminist practice. Feminist therapy practice with men, with families, and in forensic settings; feminist approaches to questions of assessment and diagnosis; feminist therapeutic applications to training and supervision; and the integration of feminist and multicultural approaches have all emerged within the 25 years since the term *feminist therapy* was first used (for a more complete discussion of many of these issues, see Brown, 1994). The modal feminist therapy situation continues to be similar to that in this video; however, a White female therapist conducts therapy with a White female client.

Feminist therapy theory has a number of underlying components, including (a) an understanding of the relationship of feminist political philosophies to therapeutic notions of change; (b) an analysis and critique of dominant cultural notions of gender, power, and authority in mainstream approaches to psychotherapy; (c) a feminist vision of the nature and meaning of psychotherapy as a phenomenon within the broader social milieu; (d) concepts of normal growth and development, distress, diagnosis, boundaries, and relationship in therapy that are grounded in feminist political analysis and scholarship; (e) an ethics code of practice tied to the feminist politic of social change and the value of interpersonal relatedness; and (f) a multicultural and theoretically diverse base of scholarship and knowledge.

Feminist therapy concerns itself with the interaction of internal phenomenological reality and external social and political experience. It assumes that there is no objective, correct viewpoint on how a person should be but rather a diversity of acceptable perspectives reflecting a variety of standpoints. Instead of promoting a normative model of mental health, feminist therapy theory values the person's capacity to successfully resist assimilation into the dominant culture and to develop a sense of one's own voice and personal integrity.

Feminist theoretical understandings of distress thus focus on the ways in which certain types of life experiences disrupt people's sense of connection to themselves and their cultures and communities. It attends to the ways in which people have lost, or had taken from them, their power to know and name themselves and their experiences. The interaction of body/biology with the interpersonal milieu at the level of family, community, and culture is identified as the locus.

Feminist therapists are centrally, although not solely, interested in the ways in which gender and gendered experience inform people's understandings of their lives and serve as sources of the distress that is a catalyst for seeking therapy. Gender is seen as a socially constructed phenomenon whose meanings and expressions vary across time, place, and situation while remaining a powerful inter- and intrapersonal organizing principle. Feminist therapy also attends to the ways in which power is expressed and experienced interpersonally, and to people's complex positioning in the interpersonal matrix of various power and dominance hierarchies.

In the case example found in this video, it is possible to observe this attention to gendered issues via the therapist's attention to the client's gender-related experiences. The therapist also comments on how the client's experiences as a woman have been silenced, ignored, or diminished. The notion that it is important for people who have been devalued or marginalized in the dominant culture because of gender, race, class, sexual orientation, age, or disability to find their own voice and value is a common theme in feminist therapy.

A multicultural base of scholarship is central to current feminist therapy theory and practice. This is not simply to make therapy competent and accessible for people from a diversity of cultural groups. Rather, feminist therapy theorizes that knowledge about and from minority and marginalized groups in a society may provide valuable insights and understandings for working with people in dominant cultures as well. The gifts that can emerge from oppression and the prices paid for being in the dominant group are equally examined when a feminist therapist attempts to understand where an individual's distress may have originated. Feminist therapists define antiracist, anticlassist, and other forms of antioppressive perspectives as ethically necessary stances for a therapist to take. Feminist therapists are not simply multiculturally literate, but they also actively pursue an understanding of their own nonconscious participation in oppressive dominance behaviors with the goal of changing these ways of relating, both in and outside therapy.

Feminist therapists are interested in creating an egalitarian relationship between therapist and client, reflecting the feminist value for power equality within relationships. To this end, the feminist therapist looks for ways in which to empower the client while staying aware of the actual power that accrues to the therapist role. Maximal authority is given to clients to define their own sense of what the problem is, to set the goals for therapy, and to be perceived as equal partners collaborating in the process of change. In feminist therapy, therapist and client are seen as a cooperating team of experts, the therapist being expert in the facilitation of the change process and the creation of safety sufficient for that change, and the client being expert on what is right and what works well.

Although the presence of a power differential due to the roles of therapist and client is always acknowledged, this perspective on the therapy relationship also takes into account the ways in which the participants vary in their power relationships with one another in the broader social context and analyzes how these variances may affect the therapeutic process. Feminist therapy theory describes the relationship as one that thus has symbolic components that reflect these "real-world" meanings held by each party as well as more traditional understandings of transferential dynamics. The constant interplay between internal and external realities that in feminist therapy theory is held to inform the development of personality and sense of self is seen also as central to an understanding of the interpersonal and relational dynamics of psychotherapy. When clients in feminist therapy go in directions opposite from those chosen by the therapist, this deviation is not seen as "resistance" to treatment in the commonly understood sense of the word. Instead, feminist therapy construes this as the client's coming to listen more attentively to self and making self, rather than the therapist, a source of valuable authority. The only "resistance" in feminist therapy is the client's capacity, valued in feminist therapy theory, to resist dominant cultural attempts at silencing or disempowerment.

The diagnostic process in feminist therapy also diverges from that of mainstream approaches. Although formal diagnostic techniques and procedures may also be utilized, feminist therapeutic diagnostic thinking pays careful attention to social and cultural variables that may affect the ways in which a person experiences and expresses distress. Symptomatology is often perceived as the remnants of prior survival strategies utilized by the client rather than as evidence of psychopathology. In conceptualizing distress, a biopsychosocial model of risk and etiological factors is utilized by feminist therapists to achieve a complex understanding of various factors contributing to the client's difficulties.

Dr. Brown identifies her approach as "feminist therapy." What does this imply to you? More specifically, what do you expect of her? Will Dr. Brown be active or passive? Will the session be structured or unstructured? Directive or nondirective? Will it focus on the past or on the present? Will the session focus on behaviors, on thoughts, or on feel-

ings? What do you expect to be the relative balance between attention to technique versus the interpersonal interaction?

Have you, or has anyone you know, undergone feminist therapy? What was it like? Was it helpful?

Client Background and Precipitating Events

Ellen

Age: 34
Sex: Female
Race: Caucasian
Marital status: Single
Education: 3 years in BFA program to study painting
Occupation: Occasionally works in an art gallery or in an art bookstore

Parents: Father (60, district judge); mother (58, pianist). Both parents are living. Ellen described her father as "stern, politically ambitious, and a perfectionist." According to Ellen, her father took the lead role in the household—managing the finances, running the household, and rearing the children, and he looked to his wife to support his role. To Ellen, her mother always seemed "dreamy and distant."

Ellen's parents were divorced when Ellen was 12, and Ellen was raised thereafter by her father and her father's sister. It is unclear to Ellen why her parents were divorced; it felt to Ellen as if her mother "just fled." Ellen has had no communication with her mother since the divorce.

Sibling: Brother (32, journalist). Ellen has always felt very close to her brother. He is someone with whom she can share her secrets.

Six months ago, Ellen was arrested for grand larceny and possession of narcotics. A few weeks ago, she was found not guilty of grand larceny and guilty of a minor drug offense. For the drug charges, she was remanded by the court to see a psychologist. Based on a referral, Ellen made an appointment with Dr. Brown.

The arrest had occurred after what Ellen had thought was a

"success and a coup" at the art gallery at which she occasionally worked. Ellen had arranged a reception at the gallery for a new show they were hanging. Ellen often put together these openings: She had style, she had a lot of contacts in the restaurant/catering business, and she made it her business to know art collectors and other people who had the wherewithal to become art collectors.

At the party, Ellen was mixing and mingling (and "sparkling" with the help of some cocaine) while making new contacts. In the back room of the gallery, she spotted a good-size oil painting from the previous show that had not been cataloged and sent to storage. Ellen decided that this was a perfect opportunity for her. Maybe she could "borrow" the oil and try to arrange a sale for the gallery. She would show the gallery owners that she could put together a deal. On the other hand, maybe she would just pocket the money for herself.

After the opening reception, the gallery owners and the artist went out to dinner, leaving Ellen to close the gallery. She and some friends lingered at the gallery for an hour or longer, drinking wine and snorting more coke. By the time she was finally ready to leave, she had almost forgotten about the painting. On the way out, however, she remembered her "plan." She took the painting, scooped up a half-used vial of coke, and jumped in a taxi to go home.

When Ellen was arrested at her apartment later that night, she was too impaired to understand the gravity of her situation. Later, she realized the trouble she was in. "Oh my God," she thought, "I'm trapped. Everyone will know I am a fake. Things are really out of control this time. My father will find out!"

Ellen worked hard to create her image. She tried to put together the impression of the person she wanted to be—someone important, successful, wealthy, well connected. She was clever, and she worked all her angles: her background, her style, her looks. She had to tell so many lies, however, that sometimes she admitted that she did not know the truth. More and more, she feared that people were catching on that she was a fake, that she did not really have the money, the high life. Her clothes were from the best stores, but she would really only "borrow" them, leaving on the tags and bringing them back to store after she wore them to a party or on a date. She often used the gallery as her home address because it was more prestigious.

Since the court sentencing, Ellen has toyed with the idea of suicide. "The lies, the cheating, the hustle are getting to be too much." In a sense, Ellen was thankful that she was being forced to see a psychotherapist.

About 2 years ago, Ellen had been running a scam at the bookstore where she worked—running up "sales" on the register and then returning the "sales" for cash, using others' credit card numbers for purchases at other stores, and stealing from the cash register. Ellen guessed that the owners were suspicious of her because she was fired without an explanation. At the time, she felt anxiety and panic. For one thing, she could have been caught; second, she felt that she was becoming further entrenched in a complicated web of lies and scams. She wondered about seeing a therapist then, but she never considered it seriously.

About 15 years ago, when Ellen was in college, her apartment was broken into and the assailant forced her to have sex with him. At the time, Ellen was taking a lot of drugs and having sex with "just about everything that moved." When the masked assailant broke in and pushed her onto her bed, she thought she recognized him. After it was over, she did not feel that bad. She did not report the incident to the police ("Who would believe me?"), and she told no one but her brother. He suggested that she see a psychologist, but she just let it go.

What is your impression of Ellen? Do you like her? How typical or atypical are her life experiences and her current behavior?

Does she need psychotherapy?

What do you believe are the core isues for Ellen? What is the utility of these initial formulations?

What overall goals for therapy do you suggest?

Before you read the next section, what topics and issues do you think will be addressed in the initial sessions?

Process Notes From Initial Sessions

Ellen called and left a message on my office answering machine that she was seeking a therapist. Her message said that she had been referred by a friend's sister who was a graduate student in the psychology program at the institution where I supervise and that she (Ellen) had been mandated to treatment by the court because of drug-related problems. I called her back and talked with her for about 15 minutes to establish in greater detail what her concerns were and whether I might be the appropriate therapist for her. I described my time availability, my fees, and my willingness to meet with her for an initial session to see if she were comfortable with therapy. Had we decided at this point that I was not the appropriate person, I would have given her the names of three other possible therapy referrals.

At the first session, we began by having Ellen read and discuss with me the informed consent to treatment material. This five-page document outlines the client's rights and responsibilites in therapy; defines the boundaries and frame of the work regarding fees, appointment times, and the parameters of the therapist–client relationships; and gives a brief description of the feminist therapeutic approach that I use. I encouraged her, as I would any client, to take the form home to reread before finally signing and returning it to me. I also gave her some information forms to complete between the first and second sessions and return to me then. We then began a process of getting to know one another. I told Ellen that I would like to begin by getting some information from her about who she was, including some life history information as well as some of the details of the legal difficulties that had brought her into treatment. I also encouraged her to be aware of any questions she might have about me and how I approached our work together and to feel free to ask such questions now or at any other point in the therapy. Toward the end of the session, I suggested to her that she might want to consider doing an experiment of attending a Narcotics Anonymous (NA) meeting; I asked her not to act on this suggestion yet, but to simply consider and think about how she felt about this possibility.

At the second session, we continued the history-taking process. Ellen asked some questions for clarification regarding the informed consent material, with particular reference to the question of confidentiality, given that I would have to be reporting to the court on her attendance at therapy. We discussed what it meant to her that I would have this sort of power and used this as a springboard for exploring Ellen's ambivalence about being in therapy and her difficulties with perceiving herself as powerful or possessing choices in this context, given the circumstances that had required her to enter treatment. We began to explore ways in which she might begin to feel more empowered in the therapy sessions, which led to further discussion about her family of origin and the ways in which she had been powerless or silenced there. Again, we discussed the pros and cons of her possible attendance at NA meetings. I asked Ellen to observe whether, between our second and third sessions, she chose to go or not to go to an NA meeting and to pay careful attention to the way in which she engaged in this decision-making process, with particular emphasis on to whom she gave authority in her decision to go or not to go. In other words, was she doing something she wanted to do, was she trying to please me, or was she doing something that she thought would placate the court system—or some combination of these things?

Between our second and third sessions, Ellen decided to go an NA meeting. Her responses to this experience energize her exchange with me at the beginning of the session on the videotape.

Were the initial sessions as you expected?

As you read this summary of the preceding sessions, are there any areas or topics that you think should be covered but were not? What other information would you seek to assess Ellen?

Before you view the tape, what do you think will unfold in the taped session? What issues will be discussed? What will the relationship between Dr. Brown and Ellen be like?

Viewer's Notes (Space provided for your notes.)

Stimulus Questions About the Videotaped Session

In the first few minutes of the session, Dr. Brown allows the patient to take the lead in describing her week. Ellen expresses her inexperience and discomfort with introspection, and Dr. Brown inquires how it feels to be in therapy and to engage in introspection.

What are your thoughts about Dr. Brown's opening approach?

About 5 minutes into the session: Dr. Brown initiates a series of questions that shift the content (but not the affective tone) of the session, such as following up Ellen's attendance at a NA meeting and questioning her feelings about uncovering secrets.

What are your observations about the patient's response to questions? Does Ellen's response suggest what her typical style of relating to others might be?

About 7 minutes into the session: The patient makes an obvious attempt to minimize the behavioral difficulties for which she was mandated to receive psychotherapy. Dr. Brown smiles and lightly chides Ellen by saying, "Wait a minute, wait a minute. I was going to say, what's wrong with this picture?"

What are the merits and drawbacks of such a therapist response to minimization on the part of the patient?

About 9 minutes into the session: Dr. Brown asks Ellen to stop talking and to pay attention to her body, her fatigue. When Ellen begins to talk, Dr. Brown stops her, asking Ellen to "indulge the shrink." A few minutes later, Ellen attempts to talk in a hurried tone, and Dr. Brown suggests that concentrating on her tiredness must be "scary."

What is the potential value of such an intervention? Do you anticipate any change in the patient's behavior?

About 15 minutes into the session: Dr. Brown uses humorous quips throughout the session, such as "What's the matter with this picture?"; "Indulge the shrink"; and "Curses, foiled again."

Under what circumstances and for what purposes do you think they are used?

About 28 minutes into the session: Dr. Brown comments that Ellen may think that expressing her emotional pain may burden Dr. Brown and that Ellen may fear that Dr. Brown will abandon her if that happens. Dr. Brown elicits Ellen's fear and then reassures Ellen that treatment will end when Ellen wants it to end.

What are your thoughts about this sequence of exploration and reassurance?

In ending the session, Dr. Brown suggests that Ellen write or draw about "what Ellen wants" prior to the next session. This suggestion converges with Ellen's own interest in painting.

What is the potential value of this between-session task?

General Questions

Did the session progress as you anticipated? Was Ellen as you expected? Was Dr. Brown as you expected?

What are your general reactions to the session? What did you feel was effective in the therapy? What do you think were the strengths and the weaknesses of this approach?

If you were not informed that this is feminist therapy, what would you have called it? What do you think makes this distinctly feminist?

After reading about the patient and viewing this session, what are your diagnostic impressions or characterizations of Ellen's problem?

How would you proceed with Ellen's therapy? How many sessions will it take?

Therapist's Reflections on the Demonstration

Dr. Brown, I'm wondering if you could share with us your thoughts and reactions to today's demonstration?

It was fairly typical for an early session with a person like Ellen.

We begin to meet the private self and move from information exchange to the next level of relationship development. I am asking myself questions such as, What can this relationship handle? What can this tolerate?

What in this demonstration did you find was typical or representative of your work? What, if anything, was atypical and not representative of what you do?

A lot of things are very typical. I go for affect. I'm very interested in people learning to listen to themselves emotionally. One of the things that I find with a number of recovering chemically dependent women is that the chemical dependency has served a numbing function. Lots of chemically dependent women have a history similar to this client's, a history of some kind of trauma. And so I'm interested, with a person in early recovery, in assessing ego strength. Ellen has a fair amount of ego strength. She's not going to crumble if I try and get some feelings up. That was pretty typical.

I think another typical thing is that I use some humor. I'm fairly casual in some ways interpersonally, I think there's not a fine line between Laura Brown, the person, and Laura Brown, the therapist, in my speech style. I use a little bit of gentle sarcasm, a little bit of poking fun, a bit of exaggeration, to feed back to the person. My style with Ellen is fairly typical.

I also was able to respond emotionally, to feel connected, to notice this person's distress. To notice the depth of her fatigue, the depth of the sadness that she's feeling and carrying with her, to feel it in my own body. To experience it empathically is also a fairly typical piece for me.

Another thing that's usual in this therapy session is my beginning to attempt to address gender issues. The questions of relationship to parents of both genders; talking about what it means to be a woman, doing the things with her body that she wasn't entirely thrilled about; beginning to look at how she constructed her image of adult womanhood; and opening the door to a notion that there are other ways to value yourself as an adult woman besides as the object of someone's sexual interest. I was beginning that because I don't want to hit people over the head with it.

And as you think about the session, are there things that you would want the patient to be dealing with between sessions, and what would you be thinking about for the next session? What would carry over?

One of the things that I'm really aware of in this budding therapy relationship is what it means that I'm a woman in a caretaking role with this woman. What are the symbolic issues that are going to emerge here? As a feminist therapist, I'm interested in the gender issue. I'm interested in the symbolic nature of the communication of that gender issue. I'm interested in how I balance empowering and respecting this woman as an adult with not leaving her feeling abandoned the way she's felt all of her life.

I'm going to be thinking about how to communicate that combination of respect for her adult integrity and for the fact that she does come with self-knowledge, self-wisdom—maybe not good access to it, but she's got it. How do I respect that and at the same time, symbolically communicate that I am there; that I will not abandon her; that I'm not afraid of her feelings; that I don't need her to take care of me; and that I won't just disappear?

My hope is that between sessions she'll try that homework assignment to paint, write about, feel this fatigue, this sadness that we got some connection with during the session. She is ambivalent about her creativity. I want to take this thing that she feels good about and ask her to use it as a door to something that's really pretty scary territory for her. I'll be very interested to see sort of how that melding of strength and fear comes out.

Suggested Readings

Brown, L. S. (1994). *Subversive dialogues: Theory of feminist therapy.* New York: Basic Books.

Brown, L. S., & Ballou, M. (Eds.). (1992). *Personality and psychopathology: Feminist reappraisals.* New York: Guilford Press.

Brown, L. S., & Root, M. P. P. (Eds.). (1990). *Diversity and complexity in feminist therapy.* New York: Haworth.

Chesler, P. (1972). *Women and madness.* New York: Doubleday.

Comas-Diaz, L., & Greene, B. (Eds.). (1994). *Women of color and mental health.* New York: Guilford Press.

Dutton-Douglas, M. A., & Walker, L. E. A. (Eds.). (1988). *Feminist psy-*

chotherapies: Integration of therapeutic and feminist systems. Norwood, NJ: Ablex.

Jordan, J., Kaplan, A. G., Miller, J. B., Stiver, I., & Surrey, J. (1992). *Women's growth in connection: Writings from the Stone Center.* New York: Guilford Press.

Hare-Mustin, R., & Marecek, J. (Eds.). (1990). *Making a difference: Psychology and the construction of gender.* New Haven, CT: Yale University Press.

Kaschak, E. (1992). *Engendered lives.* New York: Basic Books.

Lerman, H., & Porter, N. (Eds.). (1990). *Feminist ethics in psychotherapy.* New York: Springer.

Rosewater, L. B., & Walker, L. E. A. (Eds.). (1985). *Handbook of feminist therapy: Women's issues in psychotherapy.* New York: Springer.

Weisstein, N. (1970). Kinder, kuche, kirche as scientific law: Psychology constructs the female. In R. Morgan (Ed.), *Sisterhood is powerful* (pp. 205–219). New York: Vintage.

CHAPTER 2

Ethnocultural Psychotherapy

Conducted by Lillian Comas-Díaz, PhD

About Dr. Comas-Díaz

Lillian Comas-Díaz, PhD, received her doctorate in clinical psychology from the University of Massachusetts. The Executive Director of the Transcultural Mental Health Institute in Washington, DC, she also maintains a private practice there. Dr. Comas-Díaz is the former director of the APA's Office of Ethnic Minority Affairs and the former director of the Hispanic Clinic at Yale University School of Medicine. A Fellow of the APA, Dr. Comas-Díaz is the recipient of the Committee on Women in Psychology's Award for Emerging Leader for Women in Psychology. Dr. Comas-Díaz has published extensively on the topics of ethnocultural mental health, gender and ethnic factors in psychotherapy, treatment of torture victims, international psychology, and Latino mental health. Her most recent publications include *Women of Color: Integrating Ethnic and Gender Identities into Psychotherapy* (1994) and a forthcoming volume, *Ethnocultural Psychotherapy* (in press). Dr. Comas-Díaz is Editor-in-Chief of *Cultural Diversity and Mental Health*, a journal published by Wiley.

What do you know about Dr. Comas-Díaz? What are you impressions of her work from published material, conversations with and about her, or any other sources of information?

What are your expectations of Dr. Comas-Díaz' style and behavior in conducting psychotherapy?

Synopsis of Ethnocultural Psychotherapy

Provided by Lillian Comas-Díaz, PhD

Definition

Clinical realities are negotiated by therapists and clients not merely in theoretical models but also in terms of ethnocultural and racial frameworks that are permeated by subjective and contextual denotations. These multilayered racial and ethnoculturally based denotations tend to influence both the process and outcome of psychotherapy. Indeed, the acknowledgment of ethnic, cultural, and racial factors in psychotherapy often leads to a more rapid unfolding of core problems.

Ethnocultural psychotherapy was developed by Lillian Comas-Díaz and Frederick M. Jacobsen in order to integrate human diversity into clinical practice. This systemic and eclectic approach acknowledges the concept of self as an internal ethnocultural representation. The experiences of identity conflict, dislocation and adaptation, oppression, and sociopolitical issues prevalent among and specific to many culturally diverse clients are critical considerations within this approach.

Ethnocultural psychotherapy involves the acknowledgment of process variables relevant and specific to working with many culturally diverse clients. These variables include the therapeutic relationship, identity, ethnocultural parameters of psychotherapy such as transference and countertransference, and membership in a minority or oppressed group. The recognition, recovery, and use of the client's strengths constitute central tenets in this framework.

A Systemic Empowering Approach

As an empowering approach, ethnocultural psychotherapy acknowledges the significance of power and oppression and their paradoxical effects. It aims at conscientization (increasing awareness) and transformation. Within this context, conscientization involves the awakening of consciousness; a change of mentality resulting in a realistic awareness of one's place in society; the capacity to analyze critically the causes and consequences of one's position; and taking action toward transformation (Freire, 1970). The therapeutic relationship is recognized as an essential agent of change. As such, it functions as the dialogue that facilitates the process of critical consciousness and transformation.

As a systemic empowering approach, ethnocultural psychotherapy follows a "negotiated approach to patienthood," which attends to the client's perspective (Lazare & Eisenthal, 1979). This approach, which has also been called the "customer's approach to patienthood," elicits the client's perspective of the presenting complaints and attribution of dysfunction, the goals of treatment, and the request for method of treatment (Lazare, Eisenthal, & Wasserman, 1975). The negotiated approach often facilitates cross-cultural communication, fosters a collaboration between therapist and client by resolving conflict through negotiation, enhances the therapeutic alliance by addressing the client's perspective, and empowers the client by affirming his or her reality.

Ethnocultural Parameters: Self and Other Relationships

Ethnocultural psychotherapy examines self–other relationships and the attribution of otherness. The relationship between self and other is often mediated by a power differential, where the person with less power is designated as the other. Self–other relationships are central to ethnocultural psychotherapy because culturally diverse clients often become the other as a result of being defined in relationship to another, through the projection of the not-me. Those designated as others are subjected to dichotomous thinking and objectification, where difference from the norm is defined in deficient and oppositional terms. Because otherness affects the development and maintenance of an ethnocultural identity, identity conflicts are often a presenting complaint or an underlying issue among many people of color (Atkinson, Morten, & Wing, 1979).

Ethnocultural psychotherapy acknowledges the confluence of both the therapist's and the client's realities, as well as their power differentials. Due to being the other, people of color frequently become objects of defensive projections. These defensive projections may be translated into ethnocultural parameters of psychotherapy, particularly into transference and countertransference. Within this context, ethnocultural psychotherapy identifies a number of ethnic/racial transferential and countertransferential reactions occurring within intra- and interethnocultural therapeutic dyads (Comas-

Díaz & Jacobsen, 1991). Some of the interethnocultural dyadic transferential reactions include (a) overcompliance and friendliness (frequently observed when there is a societal power differential in the client–therapist dyad); (b) denial of ethnicity and culture (avoidance of discussing any issue pertinent to ethnicity or culture); (c) mistrust and suspiciousness (unacknowledged ethnocultural differences promote mistrust and suspiciousness in the client); (d) hostility (mistrust and suspiciousness can eventually lead to hostility); and (e) ambivalence (clients may struggle with negative feelings toward their therapists while simultaneously developing an attachment to them).

The intraethnocultural dyadic transferential reactions include (a) the omniscient–omnipotent therapist (complete idealization of the therapist facilitated by ethnocultural similarity); (b) the traitor (the therapist's success is equated with betrayal and *selling out* of his or her ethnicity); (c) the autoracist (clients do not want a therapist of their own ethnocultural group because they experience negative feelings toward themselves and project them onto their ethnically similar therapist); and (d) the ambivalent (clients may feel at once comfortable with their shared ethnocultural background, but at the same time they may fear too much psychological closeness).

The interethnocultural dyadic countertransferential reactions include (a) denial of ethnocultural, racial, and gender differences; (b) the clinical anthropologist (overcuriosity about the client's culture and ethnicity); (c) guilt (reaction to societal realities dictating a lower status to people of color); (d) aggression (generated by working with clients that arouse guilt or by ignorance about them); (e) pity (expression of impotence regarding people of color in the therapeutic relationship); and (f) ambivalence (therapist's ambivalence toward the client's culture may originate with an ambivalence toward his or her own ethnicity and culture).

The intraethnocultural dyadic countertransferential reactions include (a) overidentification (can lead therapists to choose activist and supportive therapy approaches for their ethnic minority clients because of unconscious fears or overidentifications with the intrapsychic aspects of their clients' problems); (b) "Us against them" (because of shared racial and gender discrimination, the clinician attributes the client's problem solely to being a person of color or a member of an oppressed minority); (c) distancing (in order to prevent overidentification problems and getting too close, the therapist may affectively distance himself or herself from the client); (d) cultural myopia (inability to see clearly because of ethnocultural factors obscuring treatment); (e) ambivalence (the therapist's own ethnoracial ambivalence projected onto the client); (f) anger (being too ethnoculturally close to the client may uncover painful unresolved issues); (g) survivor's guilt (having escaped the fate of people of color, guilt impedes clinicians' professional growth); and (h) hope and despair (hope of improving the fate of the client and community of color alternates with despair at feeling free from survival guilt). Lillian Comas-Díaz explores ethnocultural transference during the videotaped session by asking Celeste about her feelings regarding her Hispanic/Latino ethnicity.

Ethnocultural Identity

Ethnocultural psychotherapy integrates ethnicity and culture in assessment and treatment. The ethnocultural assessment was specifically developed as both a diagnostic tool and a treatment tool for culturally diverse clients (Jacobsen, 1988). The ethnocultural assessment considers several stages that may have contributed to the development of the client's ethnocultural identity. These stages include (a) the ethnocultural heritage, which involves obtaining a history of the client's ethnocultural heritage, including genetic and biological predispositions; (b) the family myth, which focuses on the circumstances that led to the client's (or his or her multigenerational family's) decision to move to another culture; (c) the posttransition analysis, which is based on the client's intellectual and emotional perception of his or her family's ethnocultural identity in the host society since the translocation; (d) self-adjustments, which concerns the client's own perceived ethnocultural adjustment in the host culture as an individual distinct from the rest of his or her family; and (e) transference and countertransference, which call for consideration of the therapist's ethnocultural background to determine specific areas of real or potential overlap with the client's (Comas-Díaz, 1994; Comas-Díaz & Jacobsen, in press-a; Jacobsen, 1988).

Ethnocultural psychotherapy acknowledges the impact of dislocation on the client's identity using ethnocultural identification.

This process refers to clients' attribution of ethnocultural characteristics to their therapists by projecting parts of themselves (Comas-Díaz & Jacobsen, 1987). Ethnocultural identification frequently occurs spontaneously and unconsciously, as when the client attributes to the therapist certain qualities or features characteristic of his or her own ethnocultural identity. This process may be facilitated by the fact that identification is one of the chief manifestations of culture, as well as a major dynamic force in therapy.

As a form of projective identification, ethnocultural identification is expressed as negative, positive, or ambivalent valence. In cases of identity fragmentation, the therapist actively fosters the client's self-identification with the client's ethnocultural heritage and identity. In order to accomplish this, the therapist engages in three major therapeutic functions: (a) reflection, whereby the therapist "mirrors" the ethnocultural pieces of the client's fragmented self; (b) education, whereby the therapist guides the client through a reformation of ethnocultural identity; and (c) mediation, whereby the therapist helps the patient integrate his or her ethnocultural self into a consolidated sense of self (Comas-Díaz & Jacobsen, 1987).

Ethnocultural Clinical Tools

Clinical tools used in ethnocultural psychotherapy include multigenerational genograms, ethnocultural transitional maps, ethnocultural tales, and testimonies. The multigenerational genograms, or family trees, are tools for diagramming complex extended family relationships and kinship networks. Genograms emphasize the relevance of the family and ethnocultural group identity by strengthening the clients' connection with their generational, group, and historical link. Multigenerational genograms can be particularly relevant when issues of ethnicity, gender, and race are examined after a therapeutic alliance has been established (Boyd-Franklin, 1989).

The ethnocultural transitional map assesses personal, familial, and community dislocations in clients and their families, involving the collection of psychological, social, and ethnocultural data, in addition to the assessment of the individual and family developmental stages (Ho, 1987). In addition to the standard clinical interviews format, the transitional map uses photographs, albums, folklore, art, paintings, native music, and other ethnocultural data as clinical tools.

Ethnocultural tales are narratives that address the development of ethnic, racial, and gender identity as a life-story construction and resconstruction (Comas-Díaz & Jacobsen, in press-a; Howard, 1991). Because oppression often silences people's voices, the main purpose of the narrative is to validate the client's reality by listening to the story in his or her own voice. Listening to ethnocultural tales provides an understanding of the messages given to the client regarding expectations, inspirations, warnings, cherished values, roles, identity issues, family and cultural scripts, self-fulfilling prophecies, prescriptions for success and failure, meaning of life and death, and other contextual information (Comas-Díaz, 1994). Specific narrative formats used are cultural and family stories. The cultural story refers to the ethnocultural group's origins, migration, and identity (McGill, 1992). At an ethnic level, cultural stories tell the ethnocultural group's collective story of how to cope with life and how to respond to pain and problems (McGill, 1992). At the family level, the narrative is used to tell where the ancestors came from, what kind of people they were, what issues are important, and what lessons have been learned from their experience (Stone, 1988).

A special type of narrative, *testimonio* (testimony), emerged in Chile as a treatment modality for victims of political repression and trauma. Testimony validates personal experience as a basis for subjective truth and knowledge in an affirming and empowering manner (Aron, 1992). It is a first-person account of one's traumatic experiences and how these have affected the individual and the family (Cienfuegos & Monelli, 1983). It consists of a verbal journey to the past that allows the individual to transform painful experiences and identity, creating a new present and enhancing the future (Cienfuegos & Monelli, 1983). This empowering approach is extremely helpful to people who have suffered individual, multigenerational, and collective trauma, dislocation, and oppression.

Summary

Ethnocultural psychotherapy addresses essential elements that have been previously ignored in traditional theoretical orientations. Indeed, many traditional therapeutic orientations have argued that clients' racial and ethnic remarks in therapy constitute a defensive shift away from underlying conflict and that the therapist's role is to interpret them as defense and resistance.

Ethnicity and culture can touch deep, unconscious feelings in most individuals and may become targets for projection by both client and therapist, making this material more available in therapy. Acknowledging ethnocultural factors does not negate the uniqueness of individuals as reflected in the developmental, biological, structural, and contextual factors comprising their psychological makeups. By addressing ethnicity and culture, ethnocultural psychotherapy helps to catalyze major therapeutic issues such as trust, ambivalence, anger, and acceptance of disparate parts of the self.

Dr. Comas-Díaz identifies her approach as "ethnocultural psychotherapy." What does this imply to you? More specifically, what do you expect of her? Will Dr. Comas-Díaz be active or passive? Will the session be structured or unstructured? Directive or nondirective? Will it focus on the past or on the present? Will the session focus on behaviors, on thoughts, or on feelings? What do you expect to be the relative balance between attention to technique versus the interpersonal interaction?

Have you, or has anyone you know, undergone ethnocultural psychotherapy? What was it like? Was it helpful?

Client Background and Precipitating Events

Celeste

Age: 29
Sex: Female
Race/Ethnicity: Caucasian/Hispanic
Marital status: Single
Education: BA
Occupation: Feature writer for *Vanity Parade*
Parents: Father (57, attorney; American of Irish descent); mother (55, attorney; naturalized U.S. citizen, born and raised in Mexico

City). As described by Celeste, both parents are strong-willed, take-charge, confident people, with very successful professional lives. Of the two, Celeste characterizes her father as the more affable and outgoing, whereas she describes her mother as "cool, correct, and unattainable." Celeste and her father have always been very close. Celeste feels that she has never been able to get close to her mother, but she very much wants her love and affection.

Siblings: Sister (32, attorney); brother (26, concert pianist). Celeste feels close to her sister, and although they are competitive, Celeste feels they are fairly equally matched in talent, looks, and professional success. On the other hand, Celeste envies her brother's enormous musical talent and his prodigious success, and she describes her feelings for him as "something less than love." According to Celeste, her brother is "Mother's darling."

Grandparents: Paternal grandfather (82, retired attorney); paternal grandmother (81, retired physician). The paternal grandmother is very close to Celeste's father and all three grandchildren. Maternal grandfather (79, retired dentist); maternal grandmother (76, retired history professor). The maternal grandparents live in Mexico City, and they have little contact with Celeste's family.

Celeste is being seriously considered for the position of managing editor of *Vanity Parade*, and she has been working hard toward this promotion. A colleague of Celeste's, Rita, is also being considered for the position. According to Celeste, Rita is jealous of her and has been "spreading vicious, vituperative stories" about how Celeste gathers material for her stories. Rita has told a number of people that Celeste has questionable lunches with sources to get information for her successful features. Rita has labeled Celeste as a "user," a "manipulator," and a "tease."

Last weekend, Celeste was working on Sunday, and when she walked by Rita's office she noticed that Rita's door was open and her computer had been left on, with Rita logged in. Celeste went into Rita's office, "just to see what was on Rita's desk," and to shut off her computer. While glancing at Rita's desk, Celeste spotted an inter-office memo, detailing Celeste's behavior with a particularly valuable source. The memo was addressed to the hiring manager for the Managing Editor position. Celeste became furious, and she started to go through Rita's computer files to see what other "lies" she could find. While she was deleting some of Rita's files, a co-worker appeared in Rita's door. He had been watching Celeste delete files.

The next day, this incident was reported to the hiring manager for the Managing Editor position. Celeste was called into his office, and she was informed that she would not be considered for this job. He also mentioned her now questionable behavior with sources. Celeste was furious, upset, and worried. This was not the first time that her anger had caused a problem for her. Maybe she needed help.

In high school, her sister had caught her shoplifting a pair of inexpensive earrings and had told her parents. Her parents made her confess and return the earrings. She was furious at her sister. The earrings were worth only $2, and she felt that everyone had made too big an issue of it. She retaliated against her sister by destroying her favorite cashmere sweater by "inadvertently" putting it in the washer and dryer.

In college, Celeste became enraged at a teaching assistant when he suggested that her term paper appeared to contain plagiarized material. She lost her temper, berated him, called him a "toadying worm" and an "intellectual midget." The incident was resolved. Her paper was not plagiarized, but she ended up taking a grade of incomplete in the course and graduating late because she could not "work with this fool."

What is your impression of Celeste? Do you like her? How typical or atypical are her life experiences and her current behavior?

Does she need psychotherapy?

What do you believe are the core issues for Celeste? What is the utility of these initial formulations?

What overall goals for therapy do you suggest?

Before you read the next section, what topics and issues do you think will be addressed in the initial sessions?

Process Notes From Initial Sessions

The initial contact was made when Celeste called my office and left a message requesting an appointment. I returned Celeste's call and elicited information regarding referral and presenting complaints. I presented the first session as a consultation in order to discuss the client's problems and offer feedback. I informed the client that at the end of the consultation, both client and therapist decide if they want to continue working together. The consultative nature of the first session is a way of empowering the client by offering choices, according to a customer's approach to psychotherapy. Instructions as to the office's address and general administrative issues (fees, cancellation policy, etc.) were discussed during this telephone contact. I invited the client to ask questions. Celeste asked about my theoretical orientation. Celeste's telephone call lasted about 15 minutes; a typical presession telephone call, however, lasts about 10 minutes.

After exchanging basic social greetings, I began the first session by asking Celeste to discuss her reason for being there. A review of the precipitating events and an elicitation of Celeste's explanation for her problems were conducted. I began to establish rapport while addressing Celeste's presenting problem of "maybe she needed help." Celeste expressed strong ambivalence toward being in psychotherapy but agreed to try it on a weekly basis. In negotiating the clinical contract, the client and I agreed to work on understanding and managing Celeste's anger. I began a clinical assessment, recognizing Celeste's emotional status of being furious, upset, and worried, while addressing her immediate crisis. The consultation followed a single-session therapy format (Talmon, 1991) in order to bolster Celeste's strengths, explore problem solving, suggest solutions for immediate implementation, and develop a therapeutic alliance.

Between the first and second sessions, I recommended a bibliotherapy source on anger and women.

During the second session, I continued establishing rapport and conducting the clinical assessment. As part of this process, clinical management issues (e.g., emergencies, physical and neurological examinations, potential psychopharmacological consultation) were discussed. I explored Celeste's anger and anger management and examined her dysfunctional and functional responses. We agreed to a violence (toward self and others) contract (similar to a suicidality contract). Then I began to examine Celeste's significant relationships by working on her ethnocultural genogram and stages I–II of the ethnocultural assessment. During this session, I examined Celeste's family explanatory model of her situation. Special attention was paid to Celeste's family's scripts of anger, achievement, and competition.

Between the second and third sessions, I asked Celeste to continue her inventory of important relationships in her life, including family (genogram), romantic partners, friends, and work relationships.

Were the initial sessions as you expected?

As you read this summary of the preceding sessions, are there any areas or topics that you think should be covered but were not? What other information would you seek to assess Celeste?

Before you view the tape, what do you think will unfold in the taped session? What issues will be discussed? What will the relationship between Dr. Comas-Díaz and Celeste be like?

Viewer's Notes (Space provided for your notes.)

Stimulus Questions About the Videotaped Session

In the opening of the session, Celeste discusses her ambivalence about being in therapy. Dr. Comas-Díaz reflects back Celeste's doubts about therapy. Further in the discussion, Dr. Comas-Díaz reiterates the terms of the therapeutic contract.

What is the value or purpose of restating the contractual arrangement? What impact might this sequence of interventions have on Celeste's ambivalence about therapy?

About 5 minutes into the session: Dr. Comas-Díaz comments on how Celeste is dealing with affect in this session. Dr. Comas-Díaz then questions whether Celeste's current behavior is in reaction to her strong emotional experiencing in the previous session. Celeste acknowledges the truth in Dr. Coma-Díaz' observation, but Celeste adds that it is typical of her usual style. Shortly thereafter, Dr. Comas-Díaz inquires how affect was handled in Celeste's family of origin.

How does Dr. Comas-Díaz' series of questions and observations compare to a formal interpretation?

About 15 minutes into the session: Celeste expresses her anger about her colleague. Dr. Comas-Díaz reflects back Celeste's feeling, saying, "You are angry." Then, Dr. Comas-Díaz asks whether there is a connection between Celeste's present feelings and her past family relations.

What is the purpose of this intervention? What value does it serve? What are the potential advantages and disadvantages of drawing a parallel to past events and feelings?

About 20 minutes into the session: Dr. Comas-Díaz refocuses the discussion about anger to feelings of hurt. Dr. Comas-Díaz offers the formulation, "For some people, it is easier to be angry than be hurt."

What reaction do you anticipate from Celeste?

About 30 minutes into the session: At this point, Dr. Comas-Díaz switches the focus of the therapy to a discussion about Celeste's relationship with her boyfriend.

What prompted this switch of focus? Would you have done so at this point in time?

About 35 minutes into the session: Dr. Comas-Díaz suggests a possible association for Celeste's feeling toward her mother (who is Hispanic) and Dr. Comas-Díaz (also Hispanic). Celeste responds, "I don't know if that has anything to do with it."

How would you react if a patient doubted the validity of your transference interpretation?

At the close of the session, Dr. Comas-Díaz asks Celeste, "Do you think you might want to come back?"

In light of the earlier discussion about their contract, what do you think Dr. Comas-Díaz' reason might be for asking this? They continue to talk about Celeste's motivation for returning. What is the value of such a discussion?

General Questions

Did the session progress as you anticipated? Was Celeste as you expected? Was Dr. Comas-Díaz as you expected?

What are your general reactions to the session? What did you feel was effective in the therapy? What do you think were the strengths and the weaknesses of this approach?

If you were not informed that this is ethnocultural psychotherapy, what would you have called it? What do you think makes this distinctly ethnocultural?

After reading about the patient and viewing this session, what are your diagnostic impressions or characterizations of Celeste's problem?

How would you proceed with Celeste's therapy? How many sessions will it take?

Therapist's Reflections on the Demonstration

Dr. Comas-Díaz, could you tell us your impressions of and feelings about this session?

This was a very complex session in the sense that we saw several of the problems that Celeste has in terms of self-esteem, her awareness and management of failing, and her relationships. It was complex from my point of view because I was trying to develop and cement trust. Many of my interventions were geared to that. In that sense, it was a difficult session.

Can you comment a little bit about what aspects of this demonstration were typical of your usual clinical work and if there were any aspects that were atypical?

As in this demonstration, I typically follow an eclectic orientation with a systemic and an empowerment perspective—gathering data in terms of the family and work systems and their impact on the client. The way I conceptualize therapy was illustrated by the way I brought in issues about other systems such as family and work and how she reacted to that.

The fact that she's Hispanic is a variable that I tried to incorporate into my work. In the session, I was asking her about her family, her mother, and her making the connection with me, whether there's any type of transference of feelings through her mother to me. There is also the issue of my being a Hispanic woman, and how she was dealing with that, in terms of her being half-Hispanic. What I did was to open up the door for that to be an ongoing issue as part of her self-esteem.

On the basis of this session, are there any ideas or feelings that you want to bring into the next session or for which you want to be particularly watchful?

Yes, I clearly want to continue to work with her in terms of her ambivalence toward therapy, toward herself, toward me, and toward her health. Although she is here, she questions at each moment whether she should stay in therapy regardless of the contract that we made. That's one of the underlying issues because it is part of her presentation, her self-destructive behavior. The way she has learned to react to certain things is the same thing she's doing in therapy. I will continue to address issues of feelings, thoughts, and behaviors and how those three things are connected to being able to change.

Suggested Readings

Aron, A. (1992). Testimony, a bridge between psychotherapy and socio-therapy. *Women & Therapy, 13* (3), 173–189.

Atkinson, D. R., Morten, G., & Wing, S. D. (1979). *Counseling American minorities: A cross-cultural perspective.* Dubuque, IA: William & Brown.

Boyd-Franklin, N. (1989). *Black families in therapy: A multisystems approach.* New York: Guilford Press.

Cienfuegos, A. J., & Monelli, C. (1983). The testimony of political repression as a therapeutic instrument. *American Journal of Orthopsychiatry, 53,* 43–51.

Comas-Díaz, L. (1994). An integrative approach. In L. Comas-Díaz & B. Greene (Eds.), *Women of color: Integrating ethnic and gender identities in psychotherapy* (pp. 287–318). New York: Guilford Press.

Comas-Díaz, L., & Griffith, E. H. E. (Eds.). (1988). *Clinical guidelines in cross cultural mental health.* New York: Wiley.

Comas-Díaz, L., & Jacobsen, F. M. (1987). Ethnocultural identification in psychotherapy. *Psychiatry, 50* (3), 232–241.

Comas-Díaz, L., & Jacobsen, F. M. (1991). Ethnocultural transference and countertransference in the therapeutic dyad. *American Journal of Orthopsychiatry, 61* (3), 392–402.

Comas-Díaz, L., & Jacobsen, F. M. (in press-a). *Ethnocultural psychotherapy.* New York: Basic Books.

Comas-Díaz, L., & Jacobsen, F. M. (in press-b). The therapist of color and the White client dyad: Clinical implications. *Cultural Diversity and Mental Health.*

Freire, P. (1970). *Pedagogy of the oppressed.* New York: The Seabury Press.

Ho, M. H. (1987). *Family therapy with ethnic minorities.* Newbury Park, Califomia: Sage.

Howard, G. S. (1991). Culture tales: A narrative approach to thinking, cross-cultural psychology, and psychotherapy. *American Psychologist, 46,* 187–197.

Jacobsen, F. M. (1988). Ethnocultural assessment. In L. Comas-Díaz & E. H. E. Griffith (Eds.), *Clinical guidelines in cross cultural mental health.* New York: Wiley.

Lazare, A., & Eisenthal, S. (1979). A negotiated approach to the clinical encounter. In A. Lazare (Ed.), *Outpatient psychiatry: Diagnosis and treatment* (pp. 141–156). Baltimore: Williams & Wilkins.

Lazare, A., Eisenthal, S., & Wasserman, L. (1975). The customer approach to patienthood: Attending to patients' requests on a walk-in clinic. *Archives of General Psychiatry, 32,* 553–558.

McGill, D. W. (1992). The cultural story in multicultural family therapy. *Families in Society, 73,* 339–349.

McGoldrick, M., Pearce, J. K., & Giordano, J. (Eds.). *Ethnicity and family therapy.* New York: Guilford Press.

Pinderhughes, E. (1989). *Understanding race, ethnicity and power: The key to efficacy in clinical practice.* New York: The Free Press.

Stone, E. (1988). *Black sheep and kissing cousins: How our family stories shape us.* New York: Penguin Books.

Talmon, J. E. (1991). *Single session therapy.* San Francisco: Jossey-Bass.

CHAPTER 3

Short-Term Dynamic Therapy

Conducted by Donald K. Freedheim, PhD

About Dr. Freedheim

Donald K. Freedheim, PhD, is an associate professor at Case Western Reserve University. He received his doctorate in clinical psychology from Duke University and completed an internship at Boston Children's Medical Center. He served as president of the APA Division of Psychotherapy (29) and edited the Division's journal, *Psychotherapy,* for 10 years. He founded the journal *Professional Psychology* and edited the volume *History of Psychotherapy: A Century of Change* (1992) for the 100th anniversary of the APA. He has had a part-time clinical practice for more than 30 years.

What do you know about Dr. Freedheim? What are your impressions of his work from published material, conversations with and about him, or any other sources of information?

What are your expectations of Dr. Freedheim's style and behavior in conducting psychotherapy?

Synopsis of Short-Term Dynamic Therapy
Provided by Donald K. Freedheim, PhD

Interest in briefer therapies has been known throughout the history of psychotherapy (Small, 1971; Wolberg, 1965), but it was not until 1975 that the First International Symposium on Short-Term

Dynamic Psychotherapy was held in Montreal. Following the conference, many well-known therapists began to develop theories and models of short-term care, but the field was defined mainly according to the works of Malan (1976), Davanloo (1980), and Sifneos (1987). Recently, shorter term therapies have been gaining stature and popularity among both therapists and their patients, if not the third-party payers of treatment (Stern, 1993). However, the growth of briefer therapies has not been without resistance. Traditional therapists questioned the validity of abbreviated means in achieving the goals of insight and interpretations of transference as necessary components of therapeutic success.

Goals of STDT

Short-term dynamic therapy (STDT) uses the same basic principles as psychoanalytic psychotherapy but with different methods of practice and somewhat different goals. The purpose of STDT is to help the patient acquire insight into the role of past events and ongoing experiences that contribute to the presenting problems. It is not, as in traditional psychoanalysis, to change significant parts of the patient's personalty. STDT has been characterized as problem- or issue-oriented in that the focus of the therapy is on dealing with a particular complaint or issue of the patient. As the treatment proceeds, other concerns may surface, but the core issue remains the focus of treatment. If enough issues develop in the treatment, the work may move away from short-term into more traditional treatment.

Although there is wide variation in therapists' estimates of the actual time involved in STDT, most writers give the number of sessions as between 20 and 40. The actual criteria for the termination of STDT are as widely argued as for any therapeutic approach, but many therapists would let the patient's judgment as to the resolution of the issues at hand be the main guide for ending the treatment. Follow-up sessions at increasingly longer intervals are a usual practice, with phone calls to "check" on the patient not uncommon.

Process

Another area of contrast to the more traditional "couch" approaches is that an alliance with the therapist is an important aspect of the treatment process. The support of the therapist is an essential ingredient of the treatment to help the patient through painful memories or conflicts that require discussion and interpretation. The alliance is sought early in the treatment and is actively encouraged by the therapist.

In terms of the interaction between the therapist and the patient, STDT differs markedly from traditional psychoanalysis, in which the therapist remains relatively passive and refrains from direct interaction with the patient. In traditional analytic treatment, the therapist allows the transference to emerge over time, with carefully planned and often suggested interpretations offered to the patient. In STDT, the therapist actively engages the patient early in the treatment, with sympathetic encouragement, suggested or even direct interpretations, and sometimes mutually agreed therapeutic contracts to help focus on the problems at hand (Liff, 1992).

Interpretations

Early in the treatment, the therapist interprets the patient's defenses, resistance, transference, and other dynamics involved in the formation of symptoms. The therapist may confront the patient to focus on themes in the conflict situation, challenge defenses, and encourage the emergence of interpersonal conflicts contributing to symptom formation. By identifying defenses, the therapist uses interpretations to help the patient understand the role of dynamics in the formation of the symptoms as well as in the development of the treatment process.

Therapists using STDT identify thoughts and feelings of the patient that may be repressed or channelled inappropriately into actions or passivity. Such discussions can take place only within a context of trust. The patient's acceptance of interpretations may be most dependent on the relationship that is developed with the therapist. In an atmosphere of warmth, understanding, and empathy, a therapist's interpretations are more readily accepted.

Transference

Transference in the therapeutic relationship also plays an important role in the treatment process. The transference is pointed out as a natural generalization from the earlier relationship, including the anticipated loss of the therapist at the completion of the treatment. Emotional abreaction and negative reactions are encouraged and accepted, within some limits, and used to point out the relevance of the therapeutic setting to the life problems of the patient.

Responsibility

STDT encourages the patient to participate actively in the treatment process and to take responsibility for the thoughts and feelings that emerge during the intervention. The therapist's role is to guide the patient's understanding of the connections between current conflicts and their possible etiologies. Interpretation as to the sources of conflicts and feelings may help the patient to express painful and other feelings within the context of the treatment.

Because the treatment approach places heavy responsibility on the patient to deal directly with conflicts and feelings, STDT should be undertaken with fairly well-defended persons who are prepared to understand dynamics of behavior and deal with the accompanying emotional manifestations.

Active support on the part of the therapist is essential, although not sufficient to bring about the understanding and insight necessary to deal fully with the patient's inter- and intrapersonal conflicts. It is important that the therapist using STDT have a full understanding of psychodynamic principles underlying personality formation. Experience with long-term treatment, including the therapist's own psychoanalysis or extended treatment, is an important prerequisite for successful use of the intervention.

Dr. Freedheim identifies his approach as "short-term dynamic therapy." What does this imply to you? More specifically, what do you expect of him? Will Dr. Freedheim be active or passive? Will the session be structured or unstructured? Directive or nondirective? Will it focus on the past or on the present? Will the session focus on behaviors, on thoughts, or on feelings? What do you expect to be the relative balance between attention to technique versus the interpersonal interaction?

Have you, or has anyone you know, undergone short-term dynamic therapy? What was it like? Was it helpful?

Client Background and Precipitating Events

Dorothy

Age: 58
Sex: Female
Race: Caucasian
Marital status: Widowed at age 55 (married for 35 years)
Education: MS, Computer Science
Occupation: Computer consultant

Husband: Larry (died at 55, married for 35 years). Dorothy and Larry had a very close and loving relationship.

Parents: Both parents are dead; the father died 5 years ago at 75; the mother died 3 years ago at 75. Dorothy was very close to her mother. In Dorothy's words, "Next to my husband, she was my best friend." Dorothy also had a good relationship with her father.

Siblings: Sister (62). Dorothy reports that she is not close to her sister. Her sister lives in another part of the country, and they rarely communicate.

Children: Son, Adam (37, computer engineer); daughter, Ann (32, CPA); daughter-in-law, Lisa (27, PhD candidate); granddaughter (5 months).

About 2 weeks ago, Dorothy's daughter, Ann, who lives in town, stopped by one afternoon to check in on Dorothy only to find Dorothy still in her robe, the house a mess, and Dorothy sitting like a zombie staring at the TV. Neither Dorothy nor her daughter could believe the state she was in. It scared Dorothy into action, or at least enough action to call a therapist (as her daughter urged).

Dorothy had been in a slump for about 6 weeks. She had not been sleeping well, and she would swing from feeling agitated to feeling hopeless. She had no idea why. She seemed to feel worse in the evenings. By the time she went to bed, she was often feeling very bad—and this was made worse by the fact that she could sleep only about 4 hours before she would bolt awake and be unable to fall back asleep for several hours. Sometimes in the middle of the night, she would just lie in bed and brood; at other times, she would get out of bed and try to clean the house, pay bills, or do something to distract her from her thoughts. Finally, she bought some over-the-counter sleeping pills, but they did not really help much.

Three weeks before she came to Dr. Freedheim, she had planned to visit her son, Adam, and his wife, Lisa, as they had recently had their first child. Dorothy was planning to stay with Adam and Lisa for 2 weeks to help out when Lisa went back to work part-time. Dorothy had planned the trip months earlier. However, as the week of the trip approached, she began to dread going to her son's home. She felt put upon: "The way I feel, I won't be of help to anyone; I'll never be able to sleep with a baby around; I just can't *face* it!"

Feeling almost desperate, she canceled the trip at the last minute. In lieu of going to help them, she located a temporary housekeeping and nanny service and paid for one month of service, to help the couple "get it together." Having done this, Dorothy felt somewhat relieved, but overall she was feeling guilty and ashamed of her behavior, of herself, and of her thoughts and feelings. She had never let her family down; she had never shirked responsibility. She was tough; she was a do-er.

Dorothy felt as if she was sinking into despair. She was hardly sleeping; she had gained 5 pounds; and she "looked like hell." She thought, "What is wrong with me? Where will this end? This isn't who I am. I am a successful, well-groomed, active businesswoman. I didn't get this bad when my husband and my mother died. I can't go on this way. Am I losing my mind?"

In her private consulting firm, she could virtually make her own hours, but she found that she was dreading any appointments because she felt as if she did not want to see anyone. She had not worked any more than the absolute minimum in well over a month.

Dorothy recalled two other times in recent years when she had struggled with intense sadness and had to work hard to cope.

Three years ago, Dorothy's husband, Larry, died unexpectedly of a heart attack. They had had a good, solid, loving, and sexual relationship for more than 35 years. They were just beginning their golden years—they had successful careers and financial security, their kids were married and doing well, and they had their health—she thought. Then, all of a sudden, it was over.

Three weeks after Larry's death, Dorothy's mother, Barbara, was diagnosed with cancer of the liver. Five months later, Barbara was dead.

Dorothy felt as if she *should* feel that her world was crashing down, but she carried on. The first year was very difficult. She suffered from insomnia and mild depression, but she was surprised by her resilience.

When Dorothy was in graduate school, she had given birth to her daughter, Ann. After Ann was born, Dorothy had a hard time coping: She suffered from "postpartum blues." She had remained in the hospital a couple of extra days after Ann was sent home with Larry. Barbara, Dorothy's mother, came to stay with Larry, Adam, and Ann to help. After her release, Dorothy saw a medical doctor a couple of times over several months. Dorothy attributed this depression to the fact that she was overwhelmed by another interruption in her studies, a second baby, and their already strapped financial situation. Until she talked with Dr. Freedheim, she had hardly remembered that difficult time.

What is your impression of Dorothy? Do you like her? How typical or atypical are her life experiences and her current behavior?

Does she need psychotherapy?

What do you believe are the core issues for Dorothy? What is the utility of these initial formulations?

What overall goals for therapy do you suggest?

Before you read the next section, what topics and issues do you think will be addressed in the initial sessions?

Process Notes From Initial Sessions

In the first session, Dorothy related that she had been "in a slump" for about 6 weeks, not sleeping well, with swings from feeling agitated to hopeless, and she raised other issues mentioned in "Client Background and Precipitating Events." I asked whether these symptoms or other similar problems had come up in the past, and she said that she had never experienced such depression and never needed to seek help before for emotional problems. In fact, she had faced some upsets in her life (i.e., the sudden death of her husband, her mother's illness and death shortly following her husband's death) with stoicism and resilience. I had her tell me about her current work, family, interests, and general enviroment in which she lives.

I noted that she was wise and brave to come to therapy and suggested that due to the rather sudden onset of symptoms, together with her good mental health history, the prognosis was good, but that we needed to work to determine the causes and deal with the issues. I indicated that we should plan a series of weekly sessions (not too specific, as I did not want either to alarm her or to have her feel that I had all the answers), probably a dozen or so, and then see where we were with the symptoms.

In the second session, I found out how the week had gone (sleeping a little better through the night but still unable to go to work). I asked to go back into her history and learn more about the sudden death of her husband (how it disrupted their plans, her life, etc.) and about the closely ensuing death of her mother (how much she had to do after the diagnosis was made, any undue suffering, her role in making plans for the estate, etc.). I noted that within about a 2-year period, she lost three significant family members. She appeared pensive and then seemed surprised by something she had forgotten and not mentioned in the first session.

She then related the depressive feelings she had had and the difficulty in leaving the hospital after the birth of her second child, and I suggested that there might be some connection between the onset of the current depression (when planning to help out with her first grandchild) and the experience following the birth of her second child. I had her note similarities and differences and indicated that although the birth of her grandchild might not be the *cause* of the current problems, it might have been a precipitating factor.

She found many similarities between these two events, such as the disruption each caused in her plans, her general lifestyle, and the feelings of responsibility involved. The birth of her child disrupted her education and career plans. She also realized the distinct differences, but she was struck by the coincidences that had never occurred to her.

By the third session, the symptoms were a little worse, and she had had some very tough nights. She nearly called me during the week (which I encouraged, if she needed) to ask about possible medication. I noted that the noticeable changes were a clue that her feelings and behavior were in flux, possibly due to some of the discussion, memories, and feelings that we had brought up.

I also suggested that if there were a connection between the depression after her child's birth and the current one, that some other concerns might be exacerbating the present depression. I lightly suggested that the closeness of her mother's illness and death upon the heels of the loss of her husband might have interfered with some of the natural mourning process.

I suggested some homework in preparation for our next session that might help us understand the role of her husband's death in the present situation. I asked her to gather some memorabilia of her husband—pictures, letters, and so forth—and review these over the week. She might even bring some pictures into the session for us to look at together.

Dr. Freedheim further reflects on this client: In the present case example of Dorothy, the underlying dynamics contributing to the patient's withdrawal were discussed early in the treatment. Following the sudden loss of her husband, she was immediately absorbed into the caretaking of her mother. Much of the normal anger and hurt caused by her husband's untimely death was repressed, and the current depression—precipitated by the birth of a grandchild—was seen as covering the now emerging angry feelings. The triggering event for her current symptoms was the anticipated visit to her newly born granddaughter, which recalled the conflicts surrounding the birth of her own daughter. Dorothy's inhibited behavior and depressed feelings were interpreted as suppressing anger over her feelings toward her deceased husband and the guilt felt by having such feelings. Her acceptance of the interpretation was at least in part due to the trust developed in the treatment relationship.

It is anticipated that the current case would continue for at least four or five weekly sessions, and several sessions following with longer duration between visits. With the alleviation of the symptoms, a better understanding of the dynamics and conflicts contributing to the problem, the patient should complete therapy in 3 to 5 months, following approximately 15 to 20 sessions.

Were the initial sessions as you expected?

As you read this summary of the preceding sessions, are there any areas or topics that you think should be covered but were not? What other information would you seek to assess Dorothy?

Before you view the tape, what do you think will unfold in the taped session? What issues will be discussed? What will the relationship between Dr. Freedheim and Dorothy be like?

Viewer's Notes (Space provided for your notes.)

Stimulus Questions About the Videotaped Session

In the opening moments of the session, Dorothy asserts, "I find that I'm feeling rather angry toward you." Dr. Freedheim acknowledges Dorothy's comment with a noncommittal "Ahhh." Dorothy then moves away from her anger to other topics. Dr. Freedheim says, "Feelings are something we need to talk about" and "particularly the ones [feelings] about me." Dr Freedheim then moves to Dorothy's homework assignment.

At this early choice point, would you focus specifically on Dorothy's anger toward the therapist, or would you follow her lead toward other topics?

About 2 minutes into the session: Dr. Freedheim acknowledges Dorothy's completion of the homework assignment to bring in pictures of her family, including her deceased husband.

What is the role of homework in short-term dynamic psychotherapy? In your experience, does homework enhance or diminish the psychoanalytic exploration of intrapsychic conflict?

About 7 minutes into the session: Dorothy begrudgingly acknowledges her anger and resentment toward her daughter. She ponders openly, "So, I shouldn't be so angry with myself?" Dr. Freedheim responds that she could accept her anger.

At this point, how would you proceed?

About 23 minutes into the session: Dr. Freedheim repeatedly draws parallels between Dorothy's past experiences and her present feelings. These "correlations," as Dorothy calls them, also appear to operate within the therapeutic relationship when she experiences and expresses anger toward Dr. Freedheim. He reassures her that these are natural feelings and that it is okay to "beat up" on him a little.

What are your reactions about his handling her anger this way? What are some alternative ways of dealing with it?

In closing the session, Dr. Freedheim reminds the patient that Dorothy could telephone him "if things get tough." Dorothy appears comforted by Dr. Freedheim's offer. Such an offer could be construed as introducing doubt as to the patient's ability to handle things herself or as reassuring her of the therapist's continuing availability.

For which patients would such an offer be indicated or contraindicated?

Dr. Freedheim advances the formulation that Dorothy's depression acts like a blanket on her anger, a variant of the classic postulate of depression as autoaggression.

Do you agree with this formulation in this particular case? In most cases?

As demonstrated in this session, short-term dynamic psychotherapy frequently entails more overt instruction, supportive interpretations, and homework assignments than in classical psychoanalytic psychotherapy.

What might be the relative advantages or disadvantages of these two approaches, specifically for Dorothy's treatment?

General Questions

Did the session progress as you anticipated? Was Dorothy as you expected? Was Dr. Freedheim as you expected?

What are your general reactions to the session? What did you feel was effective in the therapy? What do you think were the strengths and the weaknesses of this approach?

If you were not informed that this is short-term dynamic psychotherapy, what would you have called it? What do you think makes this distinctly short-term dynamic therapy?

After reading about the patient and viewing this session, what are your diagnostic impressions or characterizations of her problem?

How would you proceed with Dorothy's therapy? How many sessions will it take?

Therapist's Reflections on the Demonstration

Dr. Freedheim, what are your impressions or feelings about this session?

It was a little more collapsed than a typical session because we had to deal with so many things. I went from one thing to another a little more rapidly than I might have under other circumstances. I thought it was a very important session for Dorothy. A lot of feelings came out on the various subjects, various topics, various issues.

Would you like to say anything more about what was typical and representative to your clinical work and what was atypical?

It was typical for me to bring out and highlight certain feelings that were expressed on certain issues that were hanging over from the past and that I didn't want to let them go. I wanted her to go through the feelings and actually express them—by crying, by actually feeling some of the anger and some of the hurt. In therapy I try to have people actually experience, during that hour, the feelings that they might have talked about, that would have happened during the week, instead of just saying for, example, "I felt very sad." It can be important sometimes to have that sadness brought into the session, so one can deal directly with it.

On the basis of this session, what might you carry over or address in the next session?

There are still quite a number of unresolved issues. In this session, I wanted to show Dorothy that I could feel, have empathy for her—feel some of the hurt and understand a lot of what she was going through. She has to deal with the anger. We go through some rehearsals so that she can deal directly with the grandchild and with her son and her daughter-in-law without without a lot of the bad feelings from the past.

In short-term therapy, you have to provide a few of the insights for her and see if they make sense to her, see if they have meaning. In that way you can speed up some of the dynamics of what would have come out normally in a more extended therapy. In a short-term dynamic therapy, you put together a few more things instead of allowing the time for the patient to put them together.

Suggested Readings

Bauer, G., & Kobos, J. C. (1987). *Brief therapy: A guide to short-term psycho-dynamic intervention.* Northvale, NJ: Jason Aronson.

Binder, J. L. (1993). Observations on the training of therapists in time-limited dynamic psychotherapy. *Psychotherapy, 30,* 592–598.

Budman, S. H. (Ed.). (1981). *Forms of brief therapy.* New York: Guilford Press.

Crits-Christoph, P., & Barber, J. (Eds). (1991). *Handbook of short-term dynamic therapy.* New York: Basic Books.

Davanloo, H. (1980). *Short-term dynamic psychotherapy.* New York: Jason Aronson.

Liff, Z. A. (1992). Psychoanalysis and dynamic techniques. In D. K. Freedheim (Ed.), *History of Psychotherapy: A century of change* (pp. 571–586). Washington, DC: American Psychological Association.

Malan, D. (1976). *Toward a validation of dynamic psychotherapy: A replication.* New York: Plenum.

Mann, J. (1973). *Time-limited psychotherapy.* Cambridge, MA: Harvard University Press.

Sifneos, P. (1987). *Short-term dynamic psychotherapy.* New York: Plenum.

Small, L. (1971). *The briefer therapies.* New York: Brunner/Mazel.

Stern, S. (1993). Managed care, brief therapy, and theraputic integrity. *Psychotherapy, 30,* 162–175.

Strupp, H. H., & Bender, J. L. (1984). *Psychotherapy in a new key: A guide to time-limited dynamic psychotherapy.* New York: Basic Books.

Wells, R. A., & Phelps, V. J. (Eds.). (1990). *Handbook of the brief psychotherapies.* New York: Plenum.

Wolberg, L. R. (Ed.). (165). *Short-term psychotherapy.* New York: Grune & Stratton.

CHAPTER 4

Cognitive–Affective Behavior Therapy

Conducted by Marvin R. Goldfried, PhD

About Dr. Goldfried

Marvin R. Goldfried, PhD, is professor of psychology and psychiatry at State University of New York (SUNY) at Stony Brook. In addition to teaching, clinical supervision, and research, he maintains a limited practice of psychotherapy in New York City. A Diplomate of the American Board of Professional Psychology, a Fellow in the APA, and editorial board member of several journals, he has written numerous articles and books. His most recent books are the *Handbook of Psychotherapy Integration* (with John C. Norcross, 1992), *Clinical Behavior Therapy* (with Gerald C. Davison, 1994), and *From Cognitive–Behavior Therapy to Psychotherapy Integration* (1995). Dr. Goldfried is cofounder of the Society for the Exploration of Psychotherapy Integration.

What do you know about Dr. Goldfried? What are your impressions of his work from published material, conversations with and about him, or any other sources of information?

What are your expectations of Dr. Goldfried's style and behavior in conducting psychotherapy?

Synopsis of Cognitive–Affective Behavior Therapy
Provided by Marvin R. Goldfried, PhD

The approach is predominantly cognitive–behavioral in orientation, but with the incorporation of contributions from experiential therapy. It is possible to incorporate elements from these different orientations by thinking of the change process as involving certain common principles. Included among these general principles of change is the facilitation of expectations that the psychotherapy will be helpful; the presence of an optimal therapeutic relationship; the offering of feedback for purposes of increasing the patient's awareness; the encouragement of corrective experiences; and the emphasis on continued reality testing, a form of "working through."

The different therapeutic orientations reflected in this demonstration may be viewed as implementing the more general principles of change. The two major orientations to psychotherapy have something unique to offer, each complementing the other. Thus, behavior therapy has developed innovative methods, such as behavioral rehearsal and assertion/expressiveness training, for increasing the likelihood of the patient's having corrective experiences between sessions. Experiential therapy has developed techniques for affective arousal, such as the two-chair technique, providing patients with a better awareness of what they want or need.

In the videotape, Dr. Goldfried attempts to increase Janet's expressiveness by helping her tune into her feelings and intentions, encouraging her to respond in accordance with these rather than with the concerns that she may have about the potential reactions of others. By starting with an experiential focus on what the patient feels and wants, the behaviorally oriented rehearsal methods may be constructed as an "inside-out" approach to assertion and expressiveness training.

Dr. Goldfried identifies his approach as "cognitive–affective behavior therapy." What does this imply to you? More specifically, what do you expect of him? Will Dr. Goldfried be active or passive? Will the session be structured or unstructured? Directive or nondirective? Will it focus on the past or on the present? Will the session focus on behaviors, on thoughts, or on feelings? What do you expect to be the relative bal-

ance between attention to technique versus the interpersonal interaction?

Have you, or has anyone you know, undergone cognitive–affective behavior therapy? What was it like? Was it helpful?

Client Background and Precipitating Events

Janet

Age: 31
Sex: Female
Race: Caucasian
Marital status: Divorced 8 years ago after a 2-year marriage
Education: 3 semesters of college, secretarial school
Occupation: Legal secretary
Siblings: None.
Children: None.
Parents: Mother (Shirley; 60); Father (Jim) died 17 years ago at 43.

Janet reports that she was her "parents' pride" and that she is often told that "she never gave her parents a moment's worry." Her father died when she was 14. He was diabetic, and he had heart disease for 10 years before he died. Jim was a very friendly, outgoing man, who showered warmth and love on both "his girls," as he called Janet and her mother. Janet returned his love. For the last 4 years of his life, she was always at his side.

Janet's mother had wanted to study at Parsons School of Design and become a fashion designer, but there was no money for her dream. Instead, she married Jim when she was 27. She had known Jim since high school, and he had always been determined to marry her. According to Janet, her mother finally just gave in. Shirley was never really satisfied with Jim—she felt that she had compromised all her hopes and dreams when she married him. Shirley now placed all her hopes and dreams for her life on Janet.

After her father died, Janet got a job at the library to help out by making some extra money. Although Janet hoped to go to college and get a BA in drama, she had to drop out after 3 semesters because she and her mother could not afford the cost of her education. Janet went to a good secretarial school.

When Janet was 21 years old, she married Sam after a 5-month courtship. Shirley was delighted by this match. Sam was everything Shirley wanted for Janet. He was 30 years old, handsome, well established, and a successful businessman. Janet tried to be "the perfect wife and homemaker," but her marriage failed after 2 years, when it was apparent to both Janet and Sam that they really had never known each other and had nothing in common. Sam filed for divorce and married another young woman 8 months after the divorce.

Janet has thought on and off about seeing a psychologist for 4 or 5 months. She has been feeling depressed about her relationships with others; she is tired of feeling frustrated and unhappy, and she wants to change. A colleague at work suggested that she see Dr. Goldfried.

Janet has been in a relationship with Larry for about 6 months. She has had many relationships since her divorce 8 years ago, but none of them lasted for more than 7 or 8 months. Often they were with married men or men who were in some way not real possibilities. Janet believes that her relationship with Larry has the potential to be a lasting relationship. In Larry, she has finally met someone with whom she feels she might be able to really open up, someone whom she can trust and to whom she might be able to show "her real self," but she doesn't know how.

Janet does not want to blow it with Larry. She wants to be able to express herself, to get angry, to tell him what she wants in the relationship. However, she cannot, and Larry is getting frustrated with Janet's inability to express her feelings. When he tries to get her to talk about herself, she shifts the conversation back to Larry. Sometimes she gets very distant, inexpressive, and removed. Sometimes she has fits of temper over small things. When she gets angry, she is afraid of her anger and often feels that it is inappropriate. She would like to share her feelings, but she is afraid of expressing what she wants. Then she is afraid of losing Larry if she fails to open up. They seem to fight about insignificant things, such as Larry's being late or his forgetting to call her. Janet says that she "feels trapped" by her inability to express her feelings, but she is afraid to "open the door."

Janet is having problems at work, too. Janet works in a very high-powered law firm as a legal secretary. She is very good at her job, and she knows it. She often works 60 to 70 hours a week. She has worked for 5 years with two attorneys with whom she has an excellent working relationship, but recently she has been assigned to a third attorney who is a problem. The new attorney for whom she works is demanding and highly controlling: He watches over her, explains things in "excruciating and needless" detail, and acts as if she cannot handle the simplest brief. At other times, he gives little instruction, expecting her to guess his expectations. Usually she tries to ignore it. Lately, however, she has been making sarcastic and inappropriate comments to him, and she feels as if she is jeopardizing her job. She knows what she wants to say to him, but she does not have the courage to talk to him face-to-face, nor does she have the courage to talk to the two other attorneys about it, although she knows they would understand. After being happy and successful at this firm for 7 years, Janet has started to think about looking for another job just to get away from this attorney.

Janet has always had a hard time expressing wants and needs. She has a hard time saying "No" to people. About 6 weeks ago, Janet's mother, without consulting her, invited Janet's aunt and uncle to visit Janet and to stay with Janet for a week. When her mother told her that Aunt Lisa and Uncle Harry were thinking about visiting, Janet did not know how to tell her mother that she was furious at her for offering her place to relatives, nor was she able to tell her aunt and uncle that it would be terribly inconvenient for them to stay with her in her small, two-bedroom condominium for a week. Instead, she told them that "it would be great to see them" when they called to see if the offer from Janet's mother was real.

There are many other times that Janet feels she "gives in" in her relationships, rather than tell someone what she really thinks or feels. Often, Janet ends up going out for drinks after work with friends who need someone to talk to, when she would rather just go home. Her routine dinner and movie with her mother on Sunday is frequently inconvenient, but she feels that her mother counts on it. As Janet describes it, her life is filled with duties and obligations, and a desire not to let anyone down.

What is your impression of Janet? Do you like her? How typical or atypical are her life experiences and her current behavior?

Does she need psychotherapy?

What do you believe are the core issues for Janet? What is the utility of these initial formulations?

What overall goals for therapy do you suggest?

Before you read the next section, what topics and issues do you think will be addressed in the initial sessions?

Process Notes From Initial Sessions

I began the first session by asking, "Tell me, what prompted you to get in contact with me at this particular time?" Janet told about her concerns with her relationship with her boyfriend.

I then asked Janet about her recent past with other men and about her marriage. Janet told about her other relationships in the 8 years since her marriage. She rarely stays in a relationship for more than 7 or 8 months, by which time it would become too strained and stressful for her. During each of Janet's relationships, she was monogamous.

Toward the end of the session, I described what would happen in therapy. I told Janet that I would spend the first two sessions and part of the third session getting to know her as a person. I informed her that by the third session I would share with her what I thought.

I described the therapeutic alliance that we would seek to achieve, which comprised three parts: (a) a bond between the patient and the therapist, in which the patient must feel comfortable and assured that the therapist is in tune with the patient and that the therapist has the patient's interests at heart; (b) establishment of the goal for the therapy; and (c) agreement about the means of therapy.

I asked Janet to complete a biographical questionnaire and to mail it back to me before our second session, and I requested that she complete the Beck Depression Inventory, which I also wanted her to mail back to me before our second session.

I saved the last 5 to 10 minutes to ask Janet if she had any questions for me. She had a few questions about my background and training, which I answered. Finally, I asked Janet if she was interested in working with me. She answered yes.

I used the information from the biographical questionnaire Janet mailed to me as a launching point for our second session. I asked her specific questions about things that stood out in her "history," such as her relationship with her father and mother, the death of her father, her previous marriage, and why she went to college for only 3 semesters. Janet told me about the financial situation after her father's death and being unable to afford to finish college. She told me about secretarial school and her work history as a highly successful legal secretary.

In the third session, Janet and I explored in greater detail her relationships with men, focusing on Larry as the initial example and her marriage and two other 8-month relationships as additional examples. I looked for themes and patterns of overlap in her experiences with men. A pattern emerged of cycling monogamous relationships.

I returned Janet to a discussion about her relationship with Larry. With a goal of slowing down the deterioration of her relationship with Larry, I suggested that I might want to have a session with Larry. Because Larry is supportive of Janet's being in therapy, Janet agreed that a meeting between Larry and me might be useful.

I then turned to a further discussion of the therapeutic alliance. I restated the need for the bond between Janet and me—a sense within her that I understand what we are discussing. I explained that we would work to establish a priority of goals for the therapy. Janet clearly identified three goals (in order): improving her relationship with Larry, eventual resolution of her interpersonal problems at work, and a better long-term relationship with her mother, if possible.

I described the process of the therapy. I explained that Janet needs to learn how to tune into what she needs and find a means of expressing those needs. We will attempt to achieve this through role playing as an imaginary rehearsal of behavior in hope of removing her barriers. I described the various "risk-taking" scenarios that Janet will act out between sessions as homework. Each role-play or risk-taking homework assignment will focus on one small step in her hierarchy of fears, based on her readiness to do so.

Were the initial sessions as you expected?

As you read this summary of the preceding sessions, are there any areas or topics that you think should be covered but were not? What other information would you seek to assess Janet?

Before you view the tape, what do you think will unfold in the taped session? What issues will be discussed? What will the relationship between Dr. Goldfried and Janet be like?

Viewer's Notes (Space provided for your notes.)

Stimulus Questions About the Videotaped Session

Dr. Goldfried opens the session by suggesting the topic he would like to discuss today, namely, Janet's relationship with her boyfriend (Larry).

What are the advantages and disadvantages of beginning a session in this manner?

About 8 minutes into the session: Dr. Goldfried asks Janet to look at her internal conflict by taking the "two sides of herself" and engaging in a two-chair dialogue.

What do you think of this technique for yourself as a way of manifesting and resolving internal conflicts?

About 18 minutes into the session: At several points in the two-chair dialogue, Janet asks Dr. Goldfried whether she should continue. Dr. Goldfried responds affirmatively.

What considerations as a therapist would you take into account in determining whether or not to maintain the two-chair dialogue? What considerations would lead you to terminate the two-chair dialogue?

About 27 minutes into the session: Dr. Goldfried chooses the empty-chair technique for Janet to rehearse an anticipated specific encounter with her boyfriend.

What other options for rehearsal and practice would you choose? What distinguishes the empty chair from the two-chair technique?

About 30 minutes into the session: At this juncture, Dr. Goldfried anticipates resistance likely to be offered by Janet's "holding-back" side during a two-chair dialogue. Dr. Goldfried then speaks to her other side.

At this choice point, why might a therapist use role playing rather than have Janet use the two-chair technique?

About 34 minutes into the session: Dr. Goldfried tape records Janet's behavioral rehearsal with her boyfriend and then plays it back to her.

What is your opinion of this audio-feedback technique? What might be its advantages and the disadvantages?

This demonstration session proceeds slowly and systematically on a single client problem.

Do the techniques borrowed from different theoretical orientations —such as the two-chair dialogue from Gestalt, rehearsal and practice from behaviorism, and empathic responses from humanistic therapy— blend cohesively toward problem resolution?

Do you experience, or do you think Janet experiences, any discontinuity as a result of integrating the varying techniques?

General Questions

Did the session progress as you anticipated? Was Janet as you expected? Was Dr. Goldfried as you expected?

What are you general reactions to the session? What did you feel was effective in the therapy? What do you think were the strengths and the weaknesses of this approach?

If you were not informed that this is cognitive–affective behavior psychotherapy, what would you have called it? What do you think makes this distinctly cognitive–affective behavior therapy?

After reading about Janet and viewing this session, what are your diagnostic impressions or characterizations of her problem?

How would you proceed with Janet's therapy? How many sessions will it take?

Therapist's Reflections on the Demonstration

Dr. Goldfried, can you tell us a little bit about your impressions or your feelings about this session?

In many respects, it felt like this was a typical session. There were a few things here and there that were different, but I felt comfortable.

How was this demonstration session typical or representative of your clinical work, and was there anything about it that was atypical?

One of the things that I noticed that was atypical had to do with the demonstration session: The client seemed to change a little bit more quickly than most people would in the third session.

The stronger part of Janet came out stronger and more quickly than it usually would with someone like Janet. Also, during the actual behavior rehearsal with the tape feedback, Janet seemed to change fairly quickly. Often it takes people a longer time to reach the point that she actually reached.

When I work this way with people, there is a combination of some methodology as well as classical behavioral methodology: the two-chair and the behavior rehearsal. The overall strategy in doing this kind of work, with somebody who's inexpressive, is something like assertiveness training. There certainly are elements in this session, but we were dealing more with emotional expressiveness than refusal. You want the person to tune into either an emotion or a desire on his or her part and have the person verbalize that without being overly inhibited about whether they're saying it the right way or what the other person is thinking or feeling.

I think it's somewhat different from the more traditional behavioral or cognitive–behavioral method in that I view it as a kind of assertiveness or expressiveness training from the inside out—that it's not just teaching clients how to say things through the tone of voice and the words to use. The real task is to learn to read clients' internal signals and what's true for them. Also, it is important to tune in to the feeling state experientially, and to when they are being honest. It is a cue to them that they're getting it right. We, as external observers, can hear or see what clients are saying when they are expressive, and we can take detailed coding or give impressionistic ratings. Clients don't monitor these. These are not salient to clients. What's salient to clients is what's going on inside them. I try to get clients not only to know what they're saying and doing but also to tune into what they're feeling. It's a subjective psychological state that may be unique to them. That becomes a desired goal, as it was in Janet's case.

On the basis of this session, what might you carry forward and address in the next session, and what would you want Janet to carry forward and address?

One of the things that I find important to do is to process success experiences, that is, to find instances where Janet was more expressive, such as the conversation with Larry that we planned for. I want to make that salient, because in a sense it's an exception to the rule.

There's a danger, based on what we know about schemas in cognitive psychology, that people overlook the exceptions. A potential therapeutic success experience could be forgotten or ignored or discounted: "Yes, I did it, but . . ." The client would not fully benefit from a success experience.

We try to spend some time talking about the success experience and how it was different. What were the thoughts that she had that were different? What was the struggle that she went through that allowed her to be more open? What were the feelings? How did she deal with her concerns about how Larry might take it? To what extent was she able to tune into what she needed to say without being overly concerned about the possible impact? And what was the impact? The ultimate goal is that the person feel positive about what she has done and feel confident about her ability to do it in the future.

Suggested Readings

Goldfried, M. R. (1995). *From cognitive–behavior therapy to psychotherapy integration.* New York: Springer.

Goldfried, M. R., & Davison, G. C. (1994). *Clinical behavior therapy.* New York: Wiley-Interscience.

Greenberg, L. S., Rice, L. N., & Elliott, R. (1993). *Facilitating emotional change.* New York: Guilford Press.

Linehan, M., Goldfried, M. R., & Goldfried, A. P. (1979). Assertion training: Skill acquisition or cognitive restructuring. *Behavior Therapy, 10,* 372–388.

Norcross, J. C., & Goldfried, M. R. (Eds.). (1992). *Handbook of psychotherapy integration.* New York: Basic Books.

Stricker, G., & Gold, J. R. (Eds.). (1993). *Comprehensive handbook of psychotherapy integration.* New York: Plenum.

Teasdale, J. D. (1993). Emotion and two kinds of meaning: Cognitive therapy and applied cognitive science. *Behaviour Research and Therapy, 31,* 339–354.

Wachtel, P. L. (1977). *Psychoanalysis and behavior therapy: Toward an integration.* New York: Basic Books.

CHAPTER 5

Process Experiential Psychotherapy

Conducted by Leslie S. Greenberg, PhD

About Dr. Greenberg

Leslie S. Greenberg, PhD, received his doctorate from York University in 1976. Currently he is professor of psychology and director of the Psychotherapy Research Centre at York University. Greenberg is past president of the Society for Psychotherapy Research and received the Early Career Contribution to Psychotherapy Research award of this society. He conducts a part-time practice and trains practitioners in individual and couples therapy. Dr. Greenberg has published extensively on the theory, research, and practice of emotionally focused and constructivist, experiential approaches to the psychotherapeutic process. Dr. Greenberg has written extensively on emotion in psychotherapy in his books *Facilitating Emotional Change: The Moment by Moment Process* (Greenberg, Rice, & Elliott, 1993) and *Emotion in Psychotherapy* (Greenberg & Safran, 1986). *Empathy and Psychotherapy* (Bohart & Greenberg, in press) is a forthcoming title to be published by the APA.

What do you know about Dr. Greenberg? What are your impressions of his work from published material, conversations with and about him, or any other sources of information?

What are your expectations of Dr. Greenberg's style and behavior in conducting psychotherapy?

Synopsis of Process Experiential Psychotherapy
Provided by Leslie S. Greenberg, PhD

The process experiential approach relies on the provision of a genuine, prizing, empathic relationship and on the therapist's being highly attuned and responsive to the client's moment-by-moment feelings and experience. Within the context of an empathic relationship, the therapist can profitably guide the client's cognitive–affective processing in certain directions.

A central issue for this treatment is achieving a balance between relational responsiveness and process directiveness and between leading and following. The aim is for the therapist and client to collaborate in exploring the client's experience and to construct new meaning.

Within the safe working environment created by the relationship conditions, the approach uses active interventions in a process-diagnostic and process-directive fashion. The approach is process-diagnostic in that the therapist listens for the emergence of markers of particular types of affective problems with which the client is currently struggling, such as splits between two parts of the self. It is process-directive in that when a marker emerges, the therapist suggests a specific in-session task to facilitate task resolution.

Five major sets of markers and tasks have been delineated:

- two-chair dialogues for the resolution of splits
- empty-chair dialogues for unfinished business
- systematic evocative unfolding for resolving problematic reactions
- focusing at markers of an unclear felt sense
- empathic affirmation at markers of vulnerability

In this approach, the therapist is viewed as an expert in how and when to facilitate particular kinds of exploration of experience but not as an expert on the content of the client's experience. Rather, clients are viewed as experts on their own experience, and therapy is a discovery-oriented process. The therapist, therefore, works to guide the client's experiential processing in different ways at different times to promote the type of cognitive and emotional processing that is likely to be most productive at that point and likely to lead ultimately to the resolution of relevant tasks.

Emotion plays a central role in this approach. Emotions are seen as organizing processes that enhance adaptation and problem solving. Accessing emotion in therapy and the promotion of further emotional processing are seen as leading to enduring change. Major barriers to healthy functioning arise from the inability to assimilate experience. Three major sources of dysfunction are (a) the inability to symbolize/internalize experience and thereby to integrate conceptual and experiential ("head and heart") processing; (b) the evocation of dysfunctional emotion schemes developed through trauma or a negative learning history that produce bad feelings and influence thought and action; and (c) the inability of emotion schemes to assimilate each other resulting in splits and disowning. Therapy involves (a) helping people attend to and symbolize internal experience, (b) restructuring emotion schemes by evoking them in treatment in order to make them accessible to new information, and (c) synthesizing evoked, schematically based experience into a unified coherent whole. Emotions are, therefore, evoked in therapy in order to help people make sense of what they feel and to promote emotional reorganization by the snythesis of previously unavailable internal resources. Descriptions of three of the major tasks follow.

Two-Chair Work for Conflict Splits

Two-chair dialogue addresses a class of processing difficulties in which two schemes or aspects of the self are in opposition, typically indicated by the verbal presentation in the session of a "split" (i.e., currently experienced conflict between the two aspects of self). Thus, a client might describe a split between a part that said he or she should "buckle down" and another part that likes to "putter around," or a split in which one part of a conflict is attributed to others, such when a client says, "My wife says I don't try hard enough, but I feel like I've done all I can."

In this task, the therapist initially helps the client to role play and explore the "critical" aspect of the self, identifying its harsh, negative evaluations of the "experiencing" aspect of the self. The experiencing part, in turn, expresses its affective reactions to the harsh criticism. As the dialogue continues, the harsh critic moves from general statements to more concrete and specific criticisms of the person or situation. In response to these criticisms, the experiencing chair begins to react in a more differentiated fashion until a new aspect of its experience is expressed. A sense of direction then emerges for the experiencer, which is expressed to the critic as a want or a need. The critic next moves to a statement of standards and values. At this point in the dialogue, the critic softens. This is followed by a negotiation or an integration between the two parts.

Empty-Chair Dialogue for Unfinished Business

This task intervention, drawn from Gestalt therapy, addresses a class of processing difficulties in which schematic emotion memories of significant others continue to trigger the reexperiencing of unresolved emotional reactions. Thus, when one thinks of the other person, bad feelings ensue. This intervention involves reexperiencing the unresolved feelings in the safety of the therapeutic environment, with the immediacy and intensity of the original situation, in order to allow the emotional expression to run its course and be restructured. The resolution of unfinished business involves a process of the client's expressing blame, complaint, or hurt to a negative other in the empty chair. The client then differentiates these feelings, often recalling and reliving a related episodic memory. Resolution involves the intense expression of a specific emotion (generally, anger or sadness) and the mobilization and expression of an associated, previously unmet need. In the enactment, in the empty chair of the significant other, resolution performances move through the expression of specific negative aspects by the other to a shift in the expression of the other either to a more affiliative or less dominant stance. Finally, resolution occurs in the self chair either by the expression of self-affirmation and self-assertion in which the other is held accountable for his or her damaging actions, or by the development by the client of a new view of the other, in which the client understands or forgives the other.

Evocative Unfolding of Problematic Reactions

This task intervention, identified in the context of client-centered therapy, addresses a class of emotional processing difficulties involving interactions with other people and external situations. The marker for this event consists of three identifiable features: (a) stimulus situation, such as, "When I heard her voice on the phone"; (b) an emotional or behavioral reaction on the part of the patient such as "I felt so scared"; and (c) and an indication that the patient views his or her own reactions as puzzling, inappropriate, or otherwise problematic, such as, "I don't know why I felt that way." In this perspective the fact that the patient is aware of a discrepancy between his or her expected reaction and the actual reaction indicates a current readiness to examine such interactions. The therapist helps the client reenter the situation by responding evocatively and helping the client focus on his or her responses to whatever was salient for the client.

When the incident is vividly reevoked in therapy and reprocessed more slowly and completely, clients are able to symbolize their experience and recognize that their reactions were a direct response to their subjective construals of the eliciting stimulus. Clients discover that their reaction was triggered by their own subjective construal of some aspect of the situation. This, in turn, stimulates further exploration, which leads to the recognition that the particular problematic reaction was an example of a broader style of functioning that is interfering with the client's meeting his or her own needs and goals.

Dr. Greenberg identifies his approach as "process experiential psychotherapy." What does this imply to you? More specifically, what do you expect of Dr. Greenberg? Will he be active or passive? Will the session be structured or unstructured? Directive or nondirective? Will it focus on the past or on the present? Will the session focus on behaviors, on thoughts, or on feelings? What do you expect to be the relative balance between attention to technique versus the interpersonal interaction?

Have you, or has anyone you know, undergone process experiential therapy? What was it like? Was it helpful?

Client Background and Precipitating Events

Todd

Age: 34
Sex: Male
Race: Caucasian
Marital status: Married for 10 years to Mary
Education: MS
Occupation: Engineer

Wife: Mary is a 34-year-old marine biologist holding a PhD. Although Todd reports that he is very proud of his wife's accomplishments, he often feels "overpowered by her," and as a result, he is sometimes overly solicitous to her.

Children: Daughter, Laura (6); son, Sam (4). Todd has a warm, loving, and playful relationship with his children.

Parents: Father (59, PhD, physicist); the mother died when Todd was 12. The parents were married for 11 years. The father did not remarry. According to Todd, his father is highly demanding and critical, with little warmth for Todd or his deceased wife. When Todd's mother was alive, his father was always highly critical of her, and he was frequently verbally abusive to her. When she died, the father shifted his criticalness and verbal abuse to Todd. "Whatever love Dad had or has, he always gave it to Eric [Todd's brother]."

Siblings: Brother (30, PhD, chemist). Todd has a very warm, loving relationship with his brother.

Todd made an appointment to see Dr. Greenberg based on a referral from his self-initiated contact with the Employee Assistance Program (EAP) at the company where he works.

Over the past 2 months, Todd has taken 15 days of "sick time" from his job, usually due to exhaustion, an inability to concentrate, and a sense that he "just could not face it." He has felt over the past 2 months that he cannot "face things at work—or anyplace for that matter." Afraid that his job might be jeopardized by all his absences, Todd talked to his supervisor about his problems. She recommended that he contact the EAP.

Todd has tried during this time to force himself to get up and go to work in spite of his increasing desire to isolate himself. He knows he should "just do it" like Mary "tells him to." However, his usual sense of duty and responsibility seems to have dissipated. Every day he feels more and more as if he is being pulled down; he just cannot push down his feelings of hopelessness and despair. He had begun to dread each new day because it only brings him a new sense of "inadequacy and a fear that I will never pull out of this."

Last month, Todd took his family on a long-planned family vacation to Disney World, but he felt as if he was just going through the motions. Both he and Mary had hoped that the change of scenery would jolt him out of his depression—that the time away from work would be good for him. However, it did not help. In fact, it was almost worse because he was supposed to be having a good time, and he felt that he had to act upbeat so as not to let down Mary and the children. He wished he could have just sent them on the trip without him. Being around people who were having fun made him feel more removed, distant, and withdrawn.

Todd has been struggling with this for at least 6 months, although the last 2 months have been the worst. His usual methods for getting rid of his bad moods have not seemed to work recently. In the past when he felt depressed, he would make mental lists of all the reasons why he was a good and decent person. He would count up all the people who needed him, who loved him, and who relied on him to stay well. Usually this bolstered him, or at least forced him to "get a grip." None of it was working.

About 8 weeks ago, Mary called his father because she thought that, if she couldn't help Todd, his father could always force him out of these moods. When his father called one day when Todd was home from work, his father started in his "usual shoot-from-the-hip, matter-of-fact way" by telling Todd that he should "snap out of it, and be a man; don't indulge your feelings; you have kids of your own now. Do you think you are still a child who can just sit home and cry?" After the call from his father, Todd "just wanted to die." He felt like he was a total washout in the eyes of both his wife and his father.

These feelings were not new—neither the feelings of inadequacy nor the feeling of being depressed.

He recalled another time when his father had mocked him and made him feel like a loser. When Todd was about 13 or 14, he went on a ski trip with his father and his brother. Todd did not want to go, but his father and brother were very excited about the trip, and Todd did not want to let them down. Todd knew that he was "awkward and clumsy," but he tried to ski anyway. He would fall down and get up, and fall down and get up, over and over. His father kept pushing him to try bigger and bigger slopes. Finally after one really painful fall, Todd just broke down and cried. "I can't do it, Dad. I am just no good at this." His father shouted at him to "buck up; don't be a quitter. Take your spills like a man for a change." Lots of people were around when his father yelled at him. He felt humiliated and diminished. The ski trip finally did come to an abrupt end when Todd fractured his arm trying to break a fall.

About a year ago, he was being considered for a good promotion. He had been groomed by his immediate supervisor for a newly created job. Mary was really counting on the extra money it would mean, and he wanted his father to be proud of him. Although he was clearly qualified for the job, and it was the obvious next step up from his position, the department chief decided to go outside of the company to hire. Todd wondered if he had been unfairly passed over, or if this was another case of his being "unable to cut the mustard." After this incident at work, Todd felt himself withdraw from his job. He felt little enthusiasm about or challenge from his projects. "Nothing turns out how I hope," Todd thought, "Always a loser. Always second best, and in second place."

What is your impression of Todd? Do you like him? How typical or atypical are his life experiences and his current behavior?

Does he need psychotherapy?

What do you believe are the core issues for Todd? What is the utility of these initial formulations?

What overall goals for therapy do you suggest?

Before you read the next section, what topics and issues do you think will be addressed in the initial sessions?

Process Notes From Initial Sessions

The client called and spoke to me, and we set up the first appointment. In this call, the fee and insurance information were discussed, and it was established that Todd viewed his concerns as an individual problem and wished to come alone to the session.

The first session began with my asking Todd what brought him in and what he would like to focus on. I then followed Todd's lead, responding empathically. Making emotional contact in the first session is emphasized over establishing a contract. Todd then related "his story," emphasizing the events of the last 2 months and his lack of energy, lack of concentration, sense of despair, and growing pessimism. He talked a little about his childhood, specifically the death of his mother and the long-standing criticalness of his father. My primary interventions were geared to establishing an empathic connection with Todd by attending to how awful his life feels to him right now. Toward the end of the session, I asked a few questions to fill in gaps in my understanding of precipitating events and of Todd's current life circumstances and also to determine whether he had consulted a physician about his depression and whether the physician had recommended a physical.

I opened the second session by inquiring about Todd's current mood and then let Todd go where his feelings and present mood took him. Todd elaborated on his sense of deteriorating conditions over the past 6 months, the failure of his previous way of coping, the disappointment at work about one year ago, and Mary's attempt to elicit his father's help with Todd 8 weeks earlier.

I continued to emphasize the affective elements of what Todd discussed, working to further strengthen the empathic connection and to build an alliance between patient and therapist. The session ended with mutual agreement that we would have two broad foci: to explore (a) Todd's feeling of inadequacy and (b) his distress about his childhood (particularly his unsatisfying relationship with his father).

We began the third session by working on Todd's feeling of inadequacy. Midway through the session, the two-chair technique was introduced, with Todd beginning the process of dialoging with his "internalized critic" around messages that "You're inadequate;

you're no good." In this session, material emerged about the ski trip when Todd was 13 years old.

Todd connected his current feelings of failure to his feelings of inadequacy as a child with his father. I helped Todd explore what it was like for him as a child in the skiing incident, using systematic evocative unfolding; this facilitated Todd's discovery of how angry he felt toward his father—then and now—for humiliating him.

Were the initial sessions as you expected?

As you read this summary of the preceding sessions, are there any areas or topics that you think should be covered but were not? What other information would you seek to assess Todd?

Before you view the tape, what do you think will unfold in the taped session? What issues will be discussed? What will the relationship between Dr. Greenberg and Todd be like?

Viewer's Notes (Space provided for your notes.)

Stimulus Questions About the Videotaped Session

Early in the session, Dr. Greenberg follows Todd's lead.

What are the advantages and disadvantages of opening precisely "where the patient is"? Where do these validations and reflections lead Todd?

About 8 minutes into the session: At this point in the session, Dr. Greenberg initiates the two-chair technique with Todd.

What would be the patient markers to initiate this technique? What other interventions could Dr. Greenberg have used at this choice point?

About 14 minutes into the session: In using this technique, the focus is on Todd's feelings—particularly his feelings concerning the situation with his wife, Mary. In the process, Dr. Greenberg does not pursue potential openings for gaining information about Todd's conflicts with his father.

What might be Dr. Greenberg's reasons for continuing with the affective work? Under what circumstances would you divert from affective work to obtain substantive content on other topics?

In the flow of the two-chair dialogue, Todd gestures by making a fist and tapping his other hand with his fist. After this gesture, Dr. Greenberg draws Todd's attention to it and questions its meaning and significance.

What are the possible effects of calling attention to this gesture after one instance? Does it facilitate emotional work?

About 30 minutes into the session: Dr. Greenberg asks Todd to repeat key emotional statements and key nonverbal behaviors.

What purposes are served by these interventions?

About 35 minutes into the session: Todd appears to be exhausted from the two-chair work.

At this point, would you continue with the two-chair work, or would you shift the direction or focus of therapy? What other directions could Dr. Greenberg pursue at this juncture?

About 45 minutes into the session: Dr. Greenberg repeatedly asks Todd to describe his physical experience by saying, "What do you feel like inside? Can you describe the sensation in your body?"

What are the pros and cons of attending to physical sensations rather than cognitions or feelings?

Throughout the session, Dr. Greenberg works to guide Todd's experiential processing in different ways at different times. Dr. Greenberg is relatively directive in telling the patient to switch chairs, what to say to the empty chair, and to exaggerate nonverbal behaviors. He does so, however, without encountering overt resistance from Todd.

What in Dr. Greenberg's manner and style facilitates this process?

In this session, Dr. Greenberg frequently prompts Todd for the expression of his feelings.

What do you think is the appropriate balance between cathartic release of past emotional pain and the encouragement of corrective behavior in the present?

General Questions

Did the session progress as you anticipated? Was Todd as you expected? Was Dr. Greenberg as you expected?

What are your general reactions to the session? What did you feel was effective in the therapy? What do you think were the strengths and the weaknesses of this approach?

If you were not informed that this is process experiential psychotherapy, what would you have called it? What do you think makes this distinctly process experiential?

After reading about Todd and viewing this session, what are your diagnostic impressions or characterizations of his problem?

How would you proceed with Todd's therapy? How many sessions will it take?

Therapist's Reflections on the Demonstration

Dr. Greenberg, could you share with us your thoughts, your reactions to the session?

Well, generally I felt pleased with it. It's a little awkward in the beginning. I'm trying to pay attention to what's going on. Sometimes I felt I was not fully attuned. Todd would get angry, and I was not quite certain what was really going on in him at the moment. But, after a while, it got to be good. When he got into more of the grief work, and "became" his mother, it seemed to really crystallize as an authentic experience.

Can you say a few words about how this session was typical and representative of your work, or atypical?

Typically, I would spend a lot more time making empathic contact with Todd, just talking with him, and interacting before I would move into an active intervention. I usually spend 15 or 20 minutes really connecting, although that could vary, depending on the presentation.

In the actual intervention, we jumped around quite a bit. There were actually three parts: He started off with a critic, he moved to talk to his father, and then he spoke to his mother. This was more active than a typical session. Also, we might not get into as much material in a third or fourth session. I would expect by a fifth or sixth session that we would be getting into material of this kind.

The general approach that I follow is what I call process-directive. There's a combination of following the client and also leading or guiding. The directing and the guiding that I was doing was fairly typical and standard. Basically, I'm following the person and really trying to be empathically attuned to his or her inner world and bring this out—paying a lot of attention to feeling.

Then I'm also listening for what we call "process markers." This is a process-diagnostic approach, as well as process-directive. I'm not diagnosing the *person* as such, but the mental or emotional states as they emerge in the moment. When a particular space arises that we've come to recognize as representing a particular kind of emotional problem—for example, a self-evaluative conflict in which one part of the self is negatively or critically evaluating the self—I would move in to do a dialogue between the two parts of the self, essentially the critic and the more experiencing part.

That's how the session started off, but we never really got to the critical voice. We shifted, or began to shift, to the unresolved anger toward his father and then the grief toward the mother. I might have waited until later in the therapy to deal with grief, until the alliance and the kind of security of the relationship was stronger so that he could relive the grief in a safer environment. It seemed so prevalent however, and it seemed appropriate to go into that at that moment.

I'm being guided somewhat by this map I have of what resolution looks like. However, I'm not in an instructional position. I am in a facilitative position. When I hear something come up, then I help guide attention toward that and help develop it. I'm waiting. I'm waiting until the missing or the longing comes up. Then, I know that it's important to go in and express and experience that feeling. Then I'm waiting until a change in position comes from, say, the parent from a critical position to a more understanding position, and then I would just help develop that. That's the basic approach, one in which I'm actually facilitating different kinds of experiential processing, or emotional processing at different times. Sometimes it's important to express a feeling more intensely. Other times it's important to focus internally and try to put words to feelings. Other times it's important to access negative cognitions that are depressagenic and so on. I'm selective, focusing on different kinds of internal processes at different times.

Is there anything from this session that you might have him attend to during the week or bring up the next week, or anything that you might particularly focus on and remember that you wanted to carry over and bring into the next session?

Generally, I wouldn't spend too much time focusing on what I want to bring into the next session. Rather, I would carry the whole experience into the next session.

There's still more grief work to be done; there's anger toward his father; and we haven't yet accessed the negative critical voice very clearly. The main thing I would have liked to have done, or to do in future sessions, is access the critical voice; I'd ask him to be more aware of that.

Given the grief work with his mother, I think I might ask him next week just in passing if he'd had any dreams during the week. Often when I go into deeper emotional work, I'm interested in what impact it has on the self and on his inner world, and is that manifested in dreams. I would just want to check his dream life, after deeper emotional work.

Suggested Readings

Daldrup, R., Beutler, L., Engle, D., & Greenberg, L. (1988). *Focused expressive psychotherapy*. New York: Guilford Press.

Gendlin, E. (1981). *Focusing* (2nd ed.). New York: Bantam Books.

Greenberg, L., & Johnson, S. (1988). *Emotionally focused approach to couples therapy*. New York: Guilford Press.

Greenberg, L., & Paivio, S. (in press). *Working with the emotions: A practical guide*. New York: Guilford Press.

Greenberg, L., Rice, L., & Elliott, R. (1993). *Facilitating emotional change: The moment by moment process*. New York: Guilford Press.

Greenberg, L., & Safran, J. (1986). *Emotion in psychotherapy*. New York: Guilford Press.

Greenberg, L., & Safran, J. (1989). Emotion in psychotherapy. *American Psychologist, 44*, 19–29.

Mahoney, M. (1991). *Human change processes: The scientific foundations of psychotherapy*. New York: Basic Books.

Perls, F., Hefferline, R., & Goodman, P., (1994). *Gestalt therapy: Excitement and growth in the human personality* (Rev. ed.). Highland, NY: Gestalt Journal Press.

Rogers, C. (1960). *A way of being*. Boston: Houghton Mifflin.

Safran, J., & Greenberg, L. (1991). *Emotion psychotherapy and change*. New York: Guilford Press.

CHAPTER 6

Effective Psychoanalytic Therapy of Schizophrenia and Other Severe Disorders

Conducted by Bertram P. Karon, PhD

About Dr. Karon

Bertram P. Karon, PhD, is a professor of clinical psychology at Michigan State University, who received his doctorate of psychopathology at Princeton. He is currently president of the Michigan Psychoanalytic Council; he is past president of the APA Division of Psychoanalysis, of Psychologists Interested in the Study of Psychoanalysis, and of the Michigan Society for Psychoanalytic Psychology. Awards Karon has received include (a) Outstanding Publication Relevant to Psychoanalysis Award (for Karon & VandenBos, *Psychotherapy of Schizophrenia: The Treatment of Choice*, 1981) (b) the Distinguished Psychoanalyst Award of the New York Society for Psychoanalytic Training, and (c) the Fowler Award for Distinguished Graduate Training, APA Graduate Students. He is an APA Fellow of Divisions 12 and 29, a Diplomate in Clinical Psychology, and the Principal Investigator, Michigan State Psychotherapy Research Project (regarding psychotherapy vs. medication for persons with schizophrenia).

What do you know about Dr. Karon? What are your impressions of his work from published material, conversations with and about him, or any other sources of information?

What are your expectations of Dr. Karon's style and behavior in conducting psychotherapy?

Synopsis of Effective Psychoanalytic Therapy of Schizophrenia and Other Severe Disorders
Provided by Bertram P. Karon, PhD

This is a psychoanalytic approach that assumes that all the symptoms are meaningful and are related to the life history as subjectively experienced. The unconscious is taken seriously, and everything that has informed psychoanalysis about human development and therapy is relevant.

Schizophrenia is a chronic terror syndrome. Patients who develop psychotic symptoms have had lives that would drive anyone "crazy." Although traumas that would precipitate psychoses in anyone may occur at any age (e.g., battlefield psychoses in World War II), most traumatic events are given their pathological significance by meanings based on earlier experiences. Typically, something happens at a very early age that changes the way later events are experienced, a later event then changes how further events are experienced, and so on. A succession of subtle events (and some that are not subtle) eventually leads to a subjective world in which a human being cannot survive. The resulting terror underlies not only acute psychotic breaks but also all schizophrenic symptoms. These represent aspects of the terror state or defenses against it.

It is necessary to create a therapeutic alliance by offering real help with what the patient perceives as the problem. The patient must feel that he or she has a therapist who is on the patient's side. Severely disturbed patients have unusual difficulty trusting the therapist; in psychoanalytic terms, they have had bad experiences with other people, and this is what is transferred to the therapist. Creating and maintaining a sufficiently positive transference to make therapy possible is a central task; it may be accomplished quickly, or it may remain the central task for a long time.

Hallucinations are understood and interpreted like dreams. Dreams and hallucinations represent disguised fulfillment of conscious, preconscious, or unconscious wishes. The patient's associations to the hallucinations are used to arrive at their meaning. Severely disturbed patients frequently give few associations, but those they do give are very helpful. Because the motivation has to be stronger to dream when one is wide awake (anyone can do it when asleep), it is usually easier to guess what the hallucinations are about.

There are four major bases for delusions. The first and foremost of these is transference to the world at large: reliving feelings, fantasies, and experiences from the past with no awareness that it is the past. The second source of delusion is the defense against pseudo-homosexual anxiety (as described by Freud in the Schreber case and which I have elaborated on in several clinical papers in the 1950s). The third basis for delusions is concepts and meanings that are idiosyncratic to the particular family in which the patient was raised. The last basis for delusion is the general human need for more or less systematic explanation of events and their causes. Schizophrenic patients have many delusional beliefs that will become apparent as psychotherapy progresses and must be addressed, analyzed, and corrected for therapy to be effective.

The more intelligent patients are more apt to develop a systematic understanding that is adequate enough to obviate the need for more deteriorated symptoms and, hence, to be diagnosed as paranoid or paranoid schizophrenic. The less intelligent are less likely to develop as functionally adequate a "paranoid system."

Because the paranoid system is not an abnormal process—but a normal process used to cope with unusual problems—it is possible for a nonfrightened, nonhumiliating therapist to share the patient's systematic understanding; respectfully call attention to inconsistencies; and helpfully supplement the patient's understanding with the therapist's knowledge of the world, of other people and, most importantly, of the workings of the human mind.

Probably the most bizarre symptom of schizophrenia is the catatonic stupor. Fromm-Reichmann reported a long time ago that catatonic patients see and hear everything that is going on around them, even though they do not react. They look like they are in a stupor, but they are not. They feel as if they will die if they move. Ratner's animal research confirmed this. Most animals are prey for some predator. Every species has a species-specific sequence of behaviors when it is under attack by a predator—sham death, cries of distress to warn the others in the group, and so on. The last stage seems to be this state of rigidity during which the animal is fully conscious but can endure great pain without reaction. When the animal goes into this catatonic-like state, most predators act as if they regard it as dead. The catatonic stupor is a life-and-species preservative strategy. The biological evidence is consistent with the clinical evidence. It is useful to reassure the catatonic patient that you will not allow anyone to kill him or her, that it is safe, and that you are on his or her side. Reiterate this message for as many sessions as is necessary.

In treating a severely disturbed patient, there are times when nothing the patient says or does seems to make sense. The therapist usually has many different ideas of what might be going on and must decide on which one to base the next communication. The therapist acts on the basis of his or her best clinical guess of what will be most helpful for the patient at that moment. Furthermore, because the patient is not communicating clearly, what the therapist does or does not do is a clinical judgment that will frequently be "off the mark." It is the reaction of the patient that guides the therapist toward a more helpful intervention. The therapist does not react to the patient on the basis of a "diagnostic category." Rather, the therapist reacts to how this particular patient is functioning at this particular moment in this particular session.

As the patient gets healthier, the patient takes a more active role in the therapy, and the process becomes like the psychoanalytic therapy of neurotics.

Dr. Karon identifies his approach as "effective psychoanalytic therapy of schizophrenia and other severe disorders." What does this imply to you? More specifically, what do you expect of him? Will Dr. Karon be active or passive? Will the session be structured or unstructured? Directive or nondirective? Will it focus on the past or on the present? Will the session focus on behaviors, on thoughts, or on feelings? What do you expect to be the relative balance between attention to technique versus the interpersonal interaction?

Have you, or has anyone you know, undergone psychoanalytic psychotherapy? What was it like? Was it helpful?

Client Background and Precipitating Events

Virginia

Age: 29
Sex: Female
Race: Caucasian
Marital status: Married for 7 years
Education: BA
Occupation: First-grade teacher
Husband: Dan (29, high school biology teacher).
Children: Two daughters, (5 and 2).
Parents: Father (51); mother (49).

Dan and Virginia met in the fall of their sophomore year in college. Virginia viewed Dan as her third boyfriend. After a chaste courtship of 3 years, they married. Both families were delighted with the marriage, which occurred after what the parents viewed as "a relaxed and wonderful 3-year courtship."

Dan reports that he and Virginia have a "good marriage." According to Dan, they "get along, seldom fight or argue," and their sex life is "average." When pushed for further description, Dan relates that they have intercourse one or two times a month. To the best of Dan's knowledge, Virginia has never had an orgasm.

Virginia generally agrees with her husband's view that they have "a good marriage." Virginia reports that her husband is a solid, reliable man who is very nice to her. She claims that he is an outstanding father.

Dan describes them as "financially comfortable," although he is becoming worried that Virginia's continuing emotional problems might cost her her job. Both Virgina and Dan report that no one at the school knows about her hospitalizations, because they both occurred in July.

Her father (Lou) is a truck driver with a high school education.

Virginia's mother (Betty) has a 10th-grade education. She was married when she was 18. Before she was pregnant with Virginia, she worked at a candy store; however, she has not worked since she was 20 (when she became pregnant with Virginia). Virginia is their only child. Lou wanted more children, but Betty did not. Betty is not very active; she prefers passive activities such as reading magazines, watching television, and knitting.

According to Virginia, her father doted on Virginia. When she was 12, her father still liked to wrestle with her and tickle her all over. Betty would try to get Lou to stop playing with Virginia in this manner, telling him that Virginia was too old for "roughhousing," but Lou always responded, "Oh, she is still my little girl." Betty would then turn to Virginia, saying, "Quit egging your father on." Virginia describes her parents as "wonderful." She often repeats, "I would be nothing without them."

A few months ago, the day after Virginia's youngest daughter's birthday party, Virginia began to get very nervous, agitated, and extremely fearful of men in terms of her daughters' and her safety. Virginia would start and jump if a man came close to her or her girls. She would grab the girls, hold them close, and order the man away. Unlike other times when she was apprehensive about her safety with men, she was even suspect of her husband. She refused to sleep in the room with him, and she made a pallet for herself on the floor of the girls' shared bedroom. This went on for several weeks before her husband had her admitted to a psychiatric hospital. She was hospitalized for 3 weeks, stabilized on medications, and discharged 2 weeks ago (on psychoactive medication).

When she was discharged a few weeks ago, the psychiatrist who had treated her in the hospital recommended that she make an appointment with Dr. Karon because the psychiatrist was familiar with Dr. Karon's work with severely disturbed patients.

At age 17, Virginia was hospitalized for the first time, after "freaking out" when a family friend touched her shoulder while complimenting her on her new haircut. Screaming, "Don't touch me," she ran around the house with her parents chasing her. Her parents tried to calm her, and they walked her to her bedroom, but she could not sleep. By 3 a.m., she was crying and shrieking about "devils with knives trying to cut her open." This behavior continued for almost 48 hours, and her parents finally brought her to the emergency room of the local psychiatric hospital on Sunday night, where she was hospitalized and treated with medications. She was released after 3 weeks, and she returned to high school. She continued to be withdrawn, but she performed adequately, receiving grades of "B," and she graduated with her class. After high school, she went on to the local college in the fall.

When Virginia was 26, just after her first daughter's second birthday, she was admitted for the second time to a psychiatric hospital. Virginia was convinced that the workmen in the neighborhood—electric company workers, trash collectors, letter carriers, and telephone linemen—were "mass murderers" who wanted to break into her house, rape and kill her, and kidnap her daughter. After locking herself and her daughter in the house for days on end with all the blinds drawn, her husband brought her to a psychiatric hospital, where she was hospitalized for 3 weeks, treated with medication, and released with continuing medication follow-up. Three months after her release, Virginia became pregnant with her second child. Once she realized she was pregnant, she stopped taking the medication, and she "got along just fine," according to Virginia.

The following information became available to Dr. Karon from hospital records:

When Virginia was 3, Lou and Betty were called to court on neglect charges. A neighbor accused Lou of allowing different male friends of his to look at and touch his naked daughter on various occasions, and possibly have intercourse with her. According to the accuser, Betty was not home on these occasions, and the men had been drinking in Lou and Betty's home. The neighbor further alleged that the 3-year-old Virginia had been given beer to drink. Lou was not directly accused of any sexual violation of Virginia. Both parents and Virginia denied that anything like this had happened. After investigation, interviewing, and psychological assessment of Virginia, the charges were dropped for lack of evidence.

When Virginia was 11, the parents were again reported for neglect. The claimed circumstances were essentially the same as in the previous charge, except that sexual intercourse was alleged to have occurred on several occasions. Virginia initially confirmed the sexual activity to a social worker, but later in the investigation she denied that anything had occurred. The case was later dropped because of the inability of the social service staff to provide confirming evidence.

Psychological tests at the time of the second charge described Virginia as in a "preborderline" condition. The psychologist predicted deteriorated functioning as Virginia moved into adolescence. These predictions proved partially correct. When Virginia began menstruating at 12, her academic performance deteriorated to a grade C level (after being a B+ student), and she became more shy and withdrawn. Virginia rarely spontaneously interacted with either girls or boys her age (between the ages of 12 and 15). When she was 15, Virginia again began to get better grades, and she became active in the science club and on the school newspaper and yearbook. Throughout her middle adolescence, she was seen as a "loner" and did not date.

What is your impression of Virginia? Do you like her? How typical or atypical are her life experiences and her current behavior?

Does she need psychotherapy?

What do you believe are the core issues for Virginia? What is the utility of these initial formulations?

What overall goals for therapy do you suggest?

Before you read the next section, what topics and issues do you think will be addressed in the initial sessions?

Process Notes From Initial Sessions

In this case, a referring psychiatrist initially called me about the patient. The psychiatrist felt that the patient had potential but that her prognosis would be poor with the kind of treatment and follow-up usual in that hospital. I told him to have the patient or her husband call. Virginia herself called. She seemed desperate, did not think she would get an appointment (despite the contrary information from the referring psychiatrist), and was relieved to make an appointment.

In the first session, I began by asking, "What's wrong, how can I help you?" Virginia said that she had been recently hospitalized for the third time. I said, "And you don't want to be hospitalized again." She agreed. "Hospitals are lousy places to live," I stated. She agreed but did not elaborate.

Virginia said that she did not like the medication and that she was considering stopping. She expected to be disapproved of; however, I told her that she was the best judge of whether or not she can tolerate living without medication right now. I said that if she continued to work with me, however, the odds were that eventually she would go off the medication. "If you decide to stop the medication, that's OK. But I would like you to just skip the last dose just before you see me again, so that I can see you at your worst. And I can be here if you need me. If that works out, then you can skip two doses before the next session."

We reviewed the hospitalization history. Then I asked for more background information, asking questions such as, "How old are you?" "How far did you get in school?" "Do you have a job?" and asking relevant follow-up questions to round out details.

After we discussed her answers to questions such as these, time ran out. I said, "That's all for now. I would like to see you again. Will you be here?" Virginia said she would.

The second session I began by asking, "How are things going?"

Virginia replied, "I didn't take my medication."

"None at all?" I asked.

"No, just the last dose, like you said . . . no, actually, I just stopped."

"How are you feeling?" I asked.

"I'm scared."

"Of course you are. That's why I wanted you not to skip it until just before you saw me. Part of it is that you have been taking the medication and there is a reaction to stopping, so that you will be more scared than you were before. But part of it is that you have been scared to death for a long time. What are you scared of? Do you know?"

"My husband. I am afraid he's going to hurt them."

We explored and got into Virginia's vague recall of her childhood. We reviewed again Virginia's vague memories of having been in court at age 11 or 12 because something sexual had happened to her. I reiterated that I would not let anyone kill or hurt her. She seemed less scared. Then time ran out, and I closed the session with, "See you next time."

Were the initial sessions as you expected?

As you read this summary of the preceding sessions, are there any areas or topics that you think should be covered but were not? What other information would you seek to assess Virginia?

Before you view the tape, what do you think will unfold in the taped session? What issues will be discussed? What will the relationship between Dr. Karon and Virginia be like?

Viewer's Notes (Space provided for your notes.)

Stimulus Questions About the Videotaped Session

As the session opens, Virginia is hallucinating. Dr. Karon immediately responds in an active manner—clapping his hands, moving his chair closer to Virginia, leaning toward Virginia, and speaking loudly.

What is Dr. Karon seeking to achieve by this response?

Dr. Karon then asks Virginia to reach out and touch his hand while she is hallucinating.

What do you think about his request? What might make his offer threatening or reassuring to a hallucinating patient?

About 3 minutes into the session: Virginia states that she barricaded herself in her daughter's room in order to protect her children from her husband, their father. Dr. Karon validates her positive functioning within her delusional system.

What is the purpose of Dr. Karon's entering her delusional system?

About 4 minutes into the session: Dr. Karon informs Virginia that together, they will discover everything that she needs to know, and that she does not need to know everything now, at the beginning of therapy. Dr. Karon is attempting to introduce factual historical reports about which specific detail is lacking, but which he feels is central for Virginia's self-understanding.

How does Dr. Karon help Virginia reconcile her own memories about historical events with the factual reports of these events?

About 7 minutes into the session: Earlier in the session, Dr. Karon asserts his "power" when Virginia is hallucinating by saying, "They can't get rid of me, but I can get rid of them." At this point in the session, Dr. Karon shifts the locus of power by saying, "You don't have to believe what I say, just because I say it."

What might account for this shift in Dr. Karon's stance? What are the implications for the interaction?

About 9 minutes into the session: Virginia asks Dr. Karon a factual question, "Do men like to hurt women when they have sex?"

Dr. Karon responds unhesitantly, "No." Virginia further asks Dr. Karon whether he likes to hurt his wife when they have sex. Dr. Karon again responds unhesitantly with a "No."

What might be the rationale for responding so quickly and definitely to such a personal question? Would you respond differently to the same question with this patient? With a different patient?

About 15 minutes into the session: Dr. Karon moves from discussing the specifics of contraceptive lubricants to a general statement that life is supposed to be fun and safe. Virginia responds that the hospital was safe.

How do these shifts by Dr. Karon from the specifics to the general enhance or diminish the therapeutic process?

Dr. Karon provides explicit information on the use of lubricant jelly.

What place do you think that such instruction has in psychotherapy? Under what circumstances and with what kinds of patients might you offer this instruction?

The rapid pace, early interventions, and multiple foci of the session strike some observers as moving too quickly and too intrusively with a schizophrenic patient. Others hold that such methods are appropriate for the severely disturbed patient.

What are your thoughts about Dr. Karon's approach? What do you believe to be the optimal balance between raising numerous concerns in a session and thoroughly processing those concerns in a single session?

Dr. Karon informs Virginia that he does not make or maintain any notes of the session, in response to Virginia's question about whether or not Dr. Karon will discuss her sessions with her husband.

Do you believe that this is clinically useful? What are the pros and cons? Would there be any professional or legal ramifications in not maintaining any notes?

General Questions

Did the session progress as you anticipated? Was Virginia as you expected? Was Dr. Karon as you expected?

What are your general reactions to the session? What did you feel was effective in the therapy? What do you think were the strengths and the weaknesses of this approach?

If you were not informed that this is psychoanalytic psychotherapy, what would you have called it? What do you think makes this distinctly psychoanalytic psychotherapy?

After reading about the patient and viewing this session, what are your diagnostic impressions or characterizations of Virginia's problem?

How would you proceed with Virginia's therapy? How many sessions will it take?

Therapist's Reflections on the Demonstration

Dr. Karon, what are your impressions or your feelings about this session?

It felt like therapy very quickly. It happened when I was lost and trying to do therapy, and I think the patient was involved in trying to respond—it came alive.

How is this demonstration representative of your work? Is there anything that was atypical?

It would be hard to talk about a typical patient, because patients come in at all places, they have all kinds of defenses. I would say that she represents a kind of patient that I would work with: someone who's struggling to stay in the real world where she has a lot of good functioning, and yet she's quite capable of being very sick.

She could get lost. We know what happens to people who go into the hospital three times, and they get medicated, and then afterward they come into the hospital again, and again, and again. They come to function worse and worse. Eventually, they lose their jobs. Eventually, their families get more and more despairing of them. But she hasn't reached that. She's still struggling there.

She wants to get better. She hasn't accepted the definition of herself as a chronic patient. She doesn't like how medication makes her feel. She works for a living. But she hasn't reached the point of getting social reinforcement for staying in the role of a sick person and chronic invalid.

Is the demonstration typical? No. Is it representative? Yes. There probably isn't a typical patient, because patients are varied, and, as Harry Sullivan said, nobody ever fits any of the categories that we use.

Would you care to comment about how much you talked in the session?

This is someone who has just come out of the hospital, who's had three psychotic breaks, who's coming off medication, who is just hanging on to reality. She needs structure. She doesn't need ambiguity. Ambiguity is going to scare the hell out of her because of evil things from her past. She needs a structure that's dependable. She needs a real world in which a human being can live because the real world that she's carrying with her isn't really livable.

She needs a therapist who's willing to deal with anything. She needs to know a lot about me. I have to let her know that I'm there, that I'm there to deal with anything. That I really want to see her. She needs to know that a lot. I have to create a therapist that she can hang on to and internalize. I have to create a therapy relationship that she can hang on to.

I have to create a real world that a human being is safe to live in. I have to give her the possibility that there's a real world a human being can live in safely. That there is a possibility of a therapist out there that one could trust.

As she becomes more comfortable, and as she has things she wants to talk about, I will get out of her way, and she will talk more and more. Eventually she will be doing most of the talking.

On the basis of this session, is there anything that you would carry over or want the patient to do?

I would want the patient to show up at the next hour. That's what I want the patient to do.

Suggested Readings

Benedetti, G., & Furlan, P. M. (Eds.). (1993). *The psychotherapy of schizophrenia: Effective clinical approaches—controversies, critiques and recommendations.* Seattle: Hogrefe & Huber.

Karon, B. P. (1989a). On the formation of delusions. *Psychoanalytic Psychology, 6* (2), 169–185.

Karon, B. P. (1989b). The state of the art of psychoanalysis: Science, hope, and kindness in psychoanalytic technique. *Psychoanalysis and Psychotherapy, 7,* 99–115.

Karon, B. P. (1992). The fear of understanding schizophrenia. *Psychoanalytic Psychology, 9,* 191–211.

Karon, B. P., & VandenBos, G. R., (1981). *Psychotherapy of schizophrenia: The treatment of choice.* New York: Aronson.

Karon, B. P., & Widener, A. J. (1994). Is there really a schizophrenogenic parent? *Psychoanalytic Psychology, 11,* 47–61.

VandenBos, G. R., & Karon, B. P. (1981). The treatment of severely disturbed patients, with attention to the relative cost-effectiveness of psychotherapy and medication. In B. Christiansen (Ed.), *Does psychotherapy return its costs?* (pp. 77–99). Oslo, Norway: Norwegian Research Council.

Werbart, A., & Cullberg, J. (Eds.). (1992). *Psychotherapy of schizophrenia: Facilitating and obstructive factors.* Oslo, Norway: Scandinavian University Press.

Individual Consultation From a Family Systems Perspective

Conducted by Florence W. Kaslow, PhD

About Dr. Kaslow

Florence Kaslow, PhD, received her doctorate degree from Bryn Mawr College. Dr. Kaslow is in independent practice in West Palm Beach, where she is also Director of the Florida Couples and Family Institute. Author and editor of more than 115 articles and 13 books, Dr. Kaslow was an editor of the *Journal of Marital and Family Therapy*. Dr. Kaslow has held the following positions in professional organizations: first president of the American Board of Forensic Psychology (1978–1980); past president of the APA Division of Family Psychology and the APA Division of Media Psychology; first president of the International Family Therapy Association (1987–1990); and a member of the National Academies of Practice (1987). Fellow in seven Divisions of the APA, Dr. Kaslow is also a Diplomate in Clinical, Family, and Forensic Psychology (American Board of Professional Psychology). Dr. Kaslow is the recipient of the Family Psychologist of the Year Award (1986), the APA Distinguished Contribution to Applied Psychology Award (1989), and the American Association of Marriage and Family Therapists Significant Contribution to the Field of Family Therapy Award (1991).

What do you know about Dr. Kaslow? What are your impressions of her work from published material, conversations with and about her, or any other sources of information?

What are your expectations of Dr. Kaslow's style and behavior in conducting psychotherapy?

Synopsis of Individual Consultation From a Family Systems Perspective
Provided by Florence W. Kaslow, PhD

A family systems perspective undergirds and encompasses my assessment and analysis of the attitudes and behaviors of my patients and the business or personal consultation provided. Central to this framework are such concepts as: Each person in the system influences and is impacted by every other member of the system; if one member is in pain, all members experience some reverberations; and because all share in the effect of major decisions made, it may be important to include them in the problem-solving and decision-making processes. Thus, each person's construction of his or her shared reality is deemed to be important, and it is vital that each individual have an opportunity to tell his or her story in his or her own terms. They can then consider how they want to weave the next chapters in the tapestry of their life histories, and which threads are to be separate and which are to be intertwined.

When doing a consultation with only one individual from a family systems framework, my approach is integrative (my model is called "diaclectic"), and it selectively incorporates interpretations and interventions from psychodynamic, relational/contextual, Bowenian, structural, systemic, strategic, problem-solving, cognitive–behavioral, and social constructionist approaches. When so doing, I focus on intrapsychic and interpersonal stresses and conflicts in the individual and between the self-identified patient and his or her significant others.

The first session is important to providing the structure for the psychotherapeutic work. I usually go over the intake form, raising questions based on what has been included and omitted. This is kept low-key so that the clients can become acclimated to my voice and my style, and I can listen to how they express themselves regarding seemingly neutral information-gathering questions. I can also observe nonverbal communications, as well as how they interact with me and any significant others present. I gently direct the interview but listen attentively to their questions, assumptions, conjectures, interpretations, and answers. Careful attention is paid to their version of the problem(s), what they have already done by way of trying to resolve them, and what precipitating event(s), thoughts, or feelings motivated them to seek therapy at this particular time.

Dr. Kaslow identifies her approach as "individual consultation from a family systems perspective." What does this imply to you? More specifically, what do you expect of her? Will Dr. Kaslow be active or passive? Will the session be structured or unstructured? Directive or nondirective? Will it focus on the past or on the present? Will the session focus on behaviors, on thoughts, or on feelings? What do you expect to be the relative balance between attention to technique versus the interpersonal interaction?

Have you, or has anyone you know, undergone individual therapy from a family systems perspective? What was it like? Was it helpful?

Client Background and Precipitating Events

Alan

Age: 54
Sex: Male
Race: Caucasian
Marital status: Married for 34 years to Joyce
Education: MA, economics; CPA
Occupation: CEO of accounting firm of 30 employees, founded by Alan 15 years ago
Wife: Joyce (54, director of employee benefits at a large corporation, MBA).

Alan and Joyce were married in their senior year of college. In their twenties, they lived in a "group" house with two other couples, and they were very involved in the anti–Vietnam War movement. In their thirties, they both went to school for graduate degrees, and they each took professional jobs in large corporations. Both Alan and Joyce took an active role in raising their daughter, Julie; Joyce took the more active role in raising their son, Jon. Alan described his relationship with Joyce as "passionate in our twenties and thirties; solid in our forties; and distracted and troubled in our fifties."

Children: Daughter, Julie (28, engaged to be married, CPA in Alan's company); son, Jon (20, single, student).

Parents: Father (82); mother (78).

Siblings: Brother (50); sister (48).

Alan made an appointment with Dr. Kaslow after he saw his internist for "stress headaches."

About 6 weeks ago, Alan went to his internist for a physical exam, because he was having what he labeled "debilitating stress headaches," including dizziness, visual impairment, and an ashen pallor. His physician indicated that he was "a walking time-bomb of stress and tension" and that he needed to change his work/life style. Although his internist found nothing physically wrong with Alan, he recommended exercise and consulting with a psychologist for the stress. His physician recommended Dr. Kaslow.

Alan agreed that he could probably use more exercise, and he agreed to "think about" seeing a psychologist. He probably does need to talk to someone. He is experiencing a lot of stress at work—and at home. He frequently feels like he is going to explode or drown at any minute. And, he has started having "blowups" with his daughter at the family business, which she joined 4 years earlier (after getting her MBA from Harvard).

There was always a lot a stress at work, but about 2 months ago, he "lost it" with his daughter in front of important potential business associates. Alan's company was considering an expansion of their real estate investments. Typically, they had bought industrial buildings and rented them to small electronics manufacturing companies and other "clean" industries, and they had bought a few rental properties that were doing well. Their real estate holdings were modest but very secure and provided steady income.

Alan's daughter, Julie, had been working in the business as a deputy vice president for the past 6 months. Before her promotion, Julie had learned the ropes—working with both the junior and senior accountants to learn from the "ground up."

Since her latest promotion, Julie had been headstrong on diversifying their real estate holdings. She put together a package to buy and develop some commercial property in an "up-and-coming" industrial/residential area and renovate it to contain loft dwellings, multibusiness space, and art galleries and shops. Julie made a presentation of her package to the CEO (her father) and the board of directors. Her fiance, Chris, a real estate broker, was present at the meeting.

In the middle of his daughter's presentation, Alan developed a splitting headache. He felt blinded by the pain and asked the board of directors to adjourn. When he got his daughter alone, he started "ranting and raving." "The deal is shoddy! We don't know where this money comes from. Too much is at risk here. We know nothing about developing such property, about zoning, about any of it! You and Chris want to control this business too fast, too soon!" According to Alan, he went on and on, and soon staff were politely closing doors and avoiding the hall near the executive office. Once Alan controlled himself, he felt "embarrassed, overwhelmed, and kind of scared." "Am I flipping out?"

Alan recalled two other times that he associated stress with physical pain.

The day after Julie's engagement party 6 months ago, Alan had a "sick headache." Julie had become engaged to marry a "very attractive, bright, ambitious real estate broker." Everyone thought it was a great match. In many ways, Alan had to agree he "might be good for his daughter: He has a lot of get up and go, and every family can use a smart businessman." However, Alan was somewhat concerned about Chris's "inordinate" interest in the family's business. Chris wanted to know all about the real estate holdings, the accounting firm's assets, and other investments. Alan wondered if perhaps Julie should have a prenuptial agreement to keep Chris out of the business.

When Alan expressed his concern to Julie and Joyce before the party, they went "ballistic." Julie was greatly offended and suggested that she should "maybe look for a position in another firm." Alan thought that maybe it was a mistake to be "handing over the firm to his daughter." He and Julie didn't speak for weeks. The whole incident was accompanied by extreme agitation and blinding headaches.

About 15 years ago, Alan left a lucrative position as a district manager of a major accounting firm to start his own business. He felt under tremendous financial and personal stress. Julie was in an expensive private school, and his son was just a young child. His wife was just beginning her career as an employee benefits specialist. Perhaps this was too much risk taking—too much change, too fast. He worried at the time about whether he should stick with the more secure job at the large firm.

He felt like he did not sleep for a year, and he had continual stomach problems. His doctor prescribed tranquilizers. However, he still felt overwhelmed by the uncertainty and the change.

What is your impression of Alan? Do you like him? How typical or atypical are his life experiences and his current behavior?

Does he need psychotherapy?

What do you believe are the core issues for Alan? What is the utility of these initial formulations?

What overall goals for therapy do you suggest?

Before you the read the next section, what topics and issues do you think will be addressed in the initial sessions?

Process Notes From Initial Sessions

During the first contact, by telephone, our secretary takes only the most basic information such as name, address, phone number, and reason for the call or nature of the problem. She turned this information about Alan over to me, because I handle all inquiries about treatment and consultation services.

In the second phone call, which lasted 5 to 10 minutes, I asked Alan a little more about the presenting problem to determine if it was appropriate for me to handle. I also asked who was the referring person, tried to get more data about the potential patient(s), and answered any questions he had about my education and training, degrees, and board certifications. I also mentioned my integrative treatment philosophy. I told him what my fees were and how these were to be paid, and I also explained how I handle insurance claims and reimbursement. I ended by giving directions to the office and asked that he plan to arrive 15 minutes before the scheduled appointment to fill out an intake individual/family form, which provides the basic data that I need to commence treatment.

Alan came reluctantly to the first session after a referral from his physician whom he had consulted about agitation and stress. Alan had told his personal story and provided background information about himself, his wife, and two children. He described his understanding of what had happened to him and his increasing feelings of disengagement from his family and how he viewed his problems.

Alan established that his primary goal was to reduce his level of stress and explosiveness. I explored what Alan had already done to relieve stress, and what had and had not worked. He was pessimistic that much could be done. A brief medical and medication history was elicited.

I also discussed the concept of the "symptom bearer," explaining to Alan that he seemed to be carrying the role of symptom bearer—that is, the individual bringing the problems in for treatment—for his larger family system. I briefly oriented Alan to family systems theory, particularly indicating that if one member of the family unit is experiencing pain, it reverberates throughout the system and all experience some distress. He agreed that probably they were all experiencing some turmoil and turbulence.

I explained that when using this approach, one considers the dynamics and needs of the self (individual), the system (or family), and society (as represented in business/work, in Alan's case), and that we would be exploring Alan's problems from these multiple foci: individual-based; family-based; and business-based. I further explained that consultation occurs in and through all levels of the "system." He seemed intrigued by these ideas but cautious about dealing with anything other that the stress he was experiencing and wanted to attribute it to a physiological problem. Two contracts were signed: one regarding confidentiality, limits to confidentiality, and other conditions of treatment; and the other regarding payment of fees.

I opened the second session with a query about how Alan reacted to the first session and what he had been thinking about and feeling, since that is relevant to his reasons for seeking consultation at this time. I followed up as to whether he wrote out his goals, contacted a physician, and attended to other things about which we had agreed. I then asked, "What seems most important for us to focus on today?" Alan further discussed other periods in his life of high anxiety, and even fear, about the unpredictability of the future. He was asked to explain what he had done in the past to cope with stressful situations, and I emphasized his various successes. I began to mention further strategies for stress reduction, including an exercise program, minivacations, and possible medication. The idea that perhaps his marital relationship was strained and this was adding to his stress was mentioned, and I suggested that maybe some of these issues could be addressed with his wife present.

Alan and I began to identify some emerging themes in the concerns. Alan articulated issues of loss and grief: the earlier loss of a secure job at a secure firm; the potential loss of his daughter (to a man he did not like) through marriage; the loss of youth (and the prospect of his mortality); the loss of romance in his marriage; and the future loss of status, role, control, and privilege as CEO of his own firm (if and when he retired).

Alan and I explored a series of possible interventions both at the business, which was the site of recent dissension, and with other family members. This included meeting with his wife; meeting with his daughter and future son-in-law; meeting with Alan and his daughter; and meeting with top executives at the firm as part of the family business consultation aspects of the intervention. Alan would be present during all of these meetings. We also discussed Alan's resuming tennis, thereby beginning to take some "time out" from work and focus on his right to and need for pleasurable activities.

Were the initial sessions as you expected?

As you read this summary of the preceding sessions, are there any areas or topics that you think should be covered but were not? What other information would you seek to assess Alan?

Before you view the tape, what do you think will unfold in the taped session? What issues will be discussed? What will the relationship between Dr. Kaslow and Alan be like?

Viewer's Notes (Space provided for your notes.)

Stimulus Questions About the Videotaped Session

Immediately after Dr. Kaslow greets Alan, he begins to express his anger and his concerns toward Dr. Kaslow for her suggested meeting with his work colleagues. Dr. Kaslow first reponds to Alan's feelings, "Wow," and then remarks that Alan seems to be angry with her as he is often angry with others. She then inquires about how his anger builds. Alan responds by talking about how his anger grew during the week. Dr. Kaslow responds that they have a misunderstanding in communication and clearly restates her understanding of how and why they came to be meeting and the agreed-on goals. This is a complicated sequence of opening interactions in the session.

Imagine that Alan is your patient. How would you feel and respond to Alan's beginning the session by expressing his anger toward you? How would you diagram this complicated series of implicit and explicit messages? How does this opening sequence aid in the therapeutic relationship and process?

Dr. Kaslow attempts to combine individual consultation and business consultation in the same session.

What are the potential difficulties and the potential synergies in this combination?

About 13 minutes into the session: At this point, Alan clearly articulates his concern about Chris's increasing influence on Julie—and implicitly, Alan's decreasing influence on her. Dr. Kaslow attempts to expand the discussion to other times when Alan may have experienced a decline in his influence on Julie. Alan chooses to further elaborate on his discomfort with Chris.

What do you do when you wish to move a patient to a broader examination of psychological issues and the patient remains anchored in his perspective?

About 25 minutes into the session: On at least three occasions, Dr. Kaslow incorporates a concrete suggestion into a question to Alan, such as "For your birthday, could you give yourself permission to enjoy life a little more?" This technique is frequently used in family systems psychotherapy.

What are the advantages of such an approach?

About 35 minutes into the session: When Alan says, "You're trying to tell me . . ." Dr. Kaslow denies that she is trying to influence Alan and states that she is asking for his thinking on the matter.

What is your reaction to this transaction? How might you have answered Alan?

About 42 minutes into the session: Dr. Kaslow hands Alan a journal with an article on succession in family business.

What role does bibliotherapy have in psychotherapy? How else might books, articles, or other suggested reading material be introduced?

At the end of this session, Dr. Kaslow extends her hand to shake hands with Alan.

Do you do this? How might different clients respond to the offer of a handshake?

General Questions

Did the session progress as you anticipated? Was Alan as you expected? Was Dr. Kaslow as you expected?

What are your general reactions to the session? What did you feel was effective in the therapy? What do you think were the strengths and the weaknesses of this approach?

If you were not informed that this is individual consultation from a family systems perspective, what would you have called it? What do you think makes this distinctly family systems therapy?

After reading about the patient and viewing this session, what are your diagnostic impressions or characterizations of Alan's problem?

How would you proceed with Alan's therapy? How many sessions will it take?

Therapist's Reflections on the Demonstration

Dr. Kaslow, would you comment a little bit about this session, what you thought about it, how it felt?

This was fairly typical of sessions I have with first-generation progenitors of family firms. Interestingly, the issues tend to be pretty much the same whether the family business is run by a man or woman, although there seems to be a little bit more conflict if it's mother–son or father–daughter than when the future successor is the same sex. Many of the issues that Alan raised are typical of what happens when the daughter is the potential successor and most of the people in the firm are uncomfortable about it.

Would you say a little bit more about your technique, the theory behind it and so forth, in terms of this demonstration? What was typical and representative? What was atypical?

Whenever I do individual therapy, my framework is the family systems framework. I'm always attending to the impact of the changes in the person I'm seeing on the family system, and the impact of the changes in others in the family on the patient I'm seeing. When there are major family life-cycle transitions happening, then the turbulence is greater. So, in Alan, we're seeing the kind of turbulence that happens. The daughter's breaking away, and she should. He's uncertain about the son. And he's facing his own mortality. Within the system, then, we look at that, both at the individual level and the family-relational, intergenerational level. When there's also the business context, that's the third level of systemic awareness. So I'm concerned about the impact of the upheaval on his personality.

You did a number of things in terms of talking about things that you were encouraging him to do between this session and the next one. Would you make any comments about that, as well as about the kinds of things that you might be thinking between sessions?

I try to range between the theories of family therapy and individual behavior in terms of an explanation of what's going on. In this case, my approach is basically psychodynamic. The intervention was being drawn from this theory using some structural techniques, some behavioral homework assignments. We talked about biofeedback, so he knew that there was some concern for the physical manifestation.

There were certainly some issues of family loyalty that would come out of contextual, organizational theory. I might give more thought to and prepare for what I might expect when he comes next time with his wife Joyce. I would think about whether he might come in angry again.

Suggested Readings

Bowen, M. (1978). *Family therapy in clinical practice*. New York: Jason Aronson.

Family Business Review. *Journal of the Family Firm Institute*. San Francisco: Jossey-Bass.

Kaslow, F. W. (1987). Marital and family therapy. In M. B. Sussman & S. K. Steinmetz (Eds.), *Handbook of marriage and the family* (pp. 835–859). New York: Plenum.

Kaslow, F. W. (Ed.). (1990). *Voices in family psychology*. Thousand Oaks, CA: Sage.

Kaslow, F. W. (1993). The lore and lure of family business. *American Journal of Family Therapy, 21*(1), 3–16.

Kaslow, F. W., & Kaslow, S. (1992). The family that works together: Special problems of family businesses. In S. Zedeck (Ed.), *Work, families and organizations* (pp. 312–361). San Francisco: Jossey-Bass.

Lidz, T. (1992). *The relevance of the family to psychoanalytic theory*. Madison, CT: International Universities Press.

Slipp, S. (1988). T*he technique and practice of object relations family therapy*. New York: Jason Aronson.

Wachtel, E. F., & Wachtel, P. L. (1986). *Family dynamics in individual psychotherapy*. New York: Guilford Press.

CHAPTER 8

Multimodal Therapy

Conducted by Arnold A. Lazarus, PhD

About Dr. Lazarus

Arnold Lazarus, PhD, earned a doctorate in clinical psychology from the University of the Witwatersrand, Johannesburg, South Africa, and after 6 years as a private practitioner, emigrated to the United States. He has taught at Stanford University, Temple University Medical School, Yale University, and Rutgers University where he has held the rank of Distinguished Professor of Psychology since 1972. Lazarus teaches in the Graduate School of Applied and Professional Psychology and has a private practice in Princeton, NJ. His professional awards include the Distinguished Service Award from the American Board of Professional Psychology, an Outstanding Contributions to Mental Health Award from the Association of Outpatient Centers of the Americas, and the Distinguished Psychologist Award from APA Division 29.

What do you know about Dr. Lazarus? What are your impressions of his work from published material, conversations with and about him, or any other sources of information?

What are your expectations of Dr. Lazarus' style and behavior in conducting psychotherapy?

Synopsis of Multimodal Therapy

Provided by Arnold A. Lazarus, PhD

The multimodal approach rests on the assumption that unless seven discrete but interactive modalities are assessed, treatment is likely to overlook significant concerns. Initial interviews and the use of a Multimodal Life History Inventory (Lazarus & Lazarus, 1991) provide an initial overview of a client's significant *b*ehaviors, *a*ffective responses, *s*ensory reactions, *i*mages, *c*ognitions, *i*nterpersonal relationships, and the need for *d*rugs and other biological interventions. The first letters yield BASIC I.D., an acronym that is easy to recall. These modalities exist in a state of reciprocal transaction and flux, connected by complex chains of behavior and other psychophysiological processes.

The therapist, usually in concert with the client, determines which specific problems across the BASIC I.D. are most salient. Whenever possible, the choice of appropriate techniques rests on well-documented research data, but multimodal therapists remain essentially flexible and are willing to improvise when necessary. They are technically eclectic, but remain theoretically consistent, drawing mainly from a broad-based social and cognitive learning theory (because its tenets are open to verification or disproof). Multimodal therapy is essentially psychoeducational and contends that many problems arise from misinformation and missing information. Thus, with most outpatients, bibliotherapy (the use of selected books for home reading) often provides a springboard for enhancing the treatment process and content.

An assiduous attempt is made to tailor the therapy to each client's unique requirements. Thus, in addition to mastering a wide range of effective techniques, multimodal counselors or clinicians address the fact that different relationship styles are also necessary. Some clients require boundless warmth and empathy, others prefer a more austere businesslike relationship. Some prefer an active trainer to a good listener (or vice versa). Because the therapeutic relationship is the soil that enables the techniques to take root, it is held that the correct method, delivered within, and geared to, the context of the client's interpersonal expectancies, will augment treatment adherence and enhance therapeutic outcomes. Another issue that requires careful scrutiny is whether individual therapy, couples therapy, family therapy, or participation in a group (or some combination of the foregoing) seems advisable. Judicious referrals are effected when necessary and feasible.

As a model for clinical practice, the multimodal approach (BASIC I.D. framework) embodies the following principles:

1. Human beings act and interact across the seven modalities.

2. These modalities are not linear but exist in a state of reciprocal transaction.

3. Accurate and thorough assessment often requires a systematic inquiry into each modality and its interaction with every other.

4. Durable treatment outcomes are more likely if significant problems throughout the BASIC I.D. are specifically corrected.

Whereas there has been a penchant in many quarters to explain psychological problems according to a fundamental underlying disturbance (e.g., faulty object relations, irrational thinking, biochemical imbalance), the multimodal view is that virtually everyone who is psychologically disturbed will display (a) conflicting or ambivalent feelings and reactions; (b) misinformation; (c) missing information; (d) maladaptive habits; (e) interpersonal inquietude; (f) issues pertaining to negative self-acceptance; (g) existential concerns; and (h) possible biological dysfunctions. Thus, in emphasizing breadth (without sacrificing depth), the multimodal approach considers it necessary to zero in on every significant area of disturbance if meaningful and long-lasting gains are to accrue.

Historically, the evolution of multimodal thinking started from a somewhat rigid behavioral perspective, to which a broad-spectrum approach was soon added (Lazarus, 1971) before finally becoming distinctly multimodal (Dryden, 1991; Lazarus, 1976, 1989). The approach was fueled mainly by follow-up inquiries that showed how durable outcomes seemed to depend largely on the acquisition of several specific coping skills across a wide range of events, and the correction of disempowering misconceptions. It seems straightforward to assume that the more useful and relevant skills and information a person learns in therapy, the less prone he or she is to relapse. ("Information" goes beyond cognitive abilities and includes anxiety management and other emotional processes.)

With most adult outpatients, the use of the 15-page Multimodal Life History Inventory (Lazarus & Lazarus, 1991) enables the clinician to pinpoint precise difficulties throughout a patient's BASIC I.D. Perusal of the completed document enables one to draw up a problem checklist (called a Modality Profile) that often serves as a "blueprint" for therapy. When problems and disturbances are relatively straightforward, it is sufficient to identify the major concerns and to focus on various methods of correcting them without having to draw up charts, lists, or profiles.

The multimodal approach rests on a social cognitive theory (Bandura, 1986) because its basic tenets are open to verification or disproof. Nevertheless, as technical eclectics, multimodal clinicians draw on effective techniques from many disciplines—without necessarily subscribing to the theories that spawned them. (Often, a technique may prove effective in spite of, rather than because of, the theory that gave rise to it.) Thus, in borrowing the empty-chair (or two-chair) technique that originated in Gestalt therapy and psychodrama, one need not subscribe to any psychodrama doctrines or Gestalt concepts. Multimodal therapists regard the empty-chair technique as a variant of role playing, and they explain its efficacy in terms of modeling, rehearsal, practice, cognitive restructuring, and other social learning theory concepts. In social and cognitive learning theory terms, the efficacy of this procedure rests on the presumed effects of cognitive restructuring, behavior rehearsal, desensitization, and the acquisition of specific interpersonal skills.

Data suggest that highly traumatic memories and flashbacks are best handled by means of exposure and stress inoculation (e.g., Foa, Rothbaum, Riggs, & Murdock, 1991), often using flooding and other extinction procedures. In less severe instances, however, we have found it unnecessary to resort to such heroic methods and prefer to use "time tripping" instead (especially with highly imaginative individuals). What is the presumed mechanism of healing? Multimodal thinkers regard it as a variant of cognitive restructuring and desensitization wherein painful memories are reprocessed and attendant affective responses are assuaged. [A procedure known as Eye-Movement Desensitization and Reprocessing (EMDR) has attracted a good deal of attention in treating posttraumatic stress disorders (Shapiro, 1989).]

The major emphasis in multimodal therapy is on flexibility. The treatment is carefully tailored to the specific needs and expectations of each individual. The explicit selection of techniques is combined with the choice of appropriate relationship styles (Lazarus, 1993). For example, on the Multimodal Life History Inventory, if a client states, "I see a good therapist as an active coach, trainer, and director," he or she is unlikely to resonate with a quiet, pensive, reflective therapist. Unless there are good reasons to do otherwise, it is important to try to meet the client's expectations. Thus, there are clients with whom multimodal therapists serve as little more than attentive listeners (because this is what that particular individual desires and requires). Others respond best to highly didactic interactions. If someone is likely to benefit from a painstaking excursion into childhood memories and encounters, a multimodal therapist will adjust his or her style accordingly. It must be strongly stressed, however, that when working in this fashion, a multimodal therapist is not practicing psychoanalysis or psychodynamic psychotherapy. The manner in which historical factors are understood and managed in multimodal therapy is distinctly different from traditional approaches (Lazarus, 1995b).

An issue that has been widely addressed in the literature on psychotherapy is the phenomenon of resistance—nonadherence to treatment, or patient noncompliance. My colleagues and I seem to encounter far less resistance than other clinicians typically report, which we attribute to the fact that we vigilantly avoid fitting the client into a preconceived treatment mode. Using the BASIC I.D. framework as a springboard for appropriate clinical interventions, we employ two procedures when therapy is not proceeding apace. They are called *bridging* and *tracking*.

Bridging is generally employed when clients appear to be avoiding issues or areas that the therapist deems important to explore or discuss. Perhaps the most typical is when the therapist inquires about feelings but receives purely intellectual (cognitive) replies. One may point out to the patient that he or she appears to be avoiding affective content, but without chiding him or her. But when this goes nowhere, it is a mistake to lock horns with the patient. Instead, it usually pays to join the client in his or her preferred modality. Thus, if purely intellectual material is forthcoming, one proceeds to discuss and examine this information. Within 5 to 10 minutes, it is usually possible to start bridging. For instance, the therapist may ask a sensory question (which is often less threatening than an emotionally laden query).

"Tell me, do you perchance notice any sensations anywhere in your body?" The patient may look puzzled. The therapist might continue, "Well, we've been talking at some length about the motivational factors behind your father's drinking. Has this discussion led to any sensations that you are aware of? Do your jaws feel tense? Is there a knot in your stomach?" In most instances, this will elicit a sensory response such as, "I seem to have a bit of a headache." Having bridged from cognition to sensation, one stays in this modality for a while. "You say you have a bit of a headache. Where exactly does your head hurt?" One dwells on the headache and inquires about attendant sensations. Within a few minutes, many patients spontaneously bridge into yet another modality. "Gee! I just had a flashback to an incident I haven't thought about for years. I can picture it so clearly." One would then explore the attendant imagery. This, in turn, often leads right into affect—which is where the therapist was heading in the first place. In other cases, by dwelling on sensory material, patients proceed directly into affective material. For example, shortly after discussing headaches and attendant sensations, a patient may say, "Come to think of it, I'm really angry with my father!" The point behind these so-called bridging maneuvers is mainly to circumvent resistance.

The other strategy that flows from the BASIC I.D. format is tracking. This refers to the "modality firing order" that clients typically employ when upsetting themselves. For instance, a woman who suffered from agoraphobia, after being asked to track and observe the sequence of events that triggered her anxiety attacks, noticed that she would typically zero-in on some unpleasant sensation such as tingling in her hands and fingers. She would then notice other untoward sensations and start thinking negative thoughts (cognition). "Perhaps this is the start of a heart attack!" This would lead to terrifying images—pictures of herself in a hospital attached to monitors, intravenous drips, and tubes. A full-blown anxiety attack would then ensue.

The awareness of her firing order S-C-I-A (sensation-cognition-imagery-affect) permitted her to interrupt the sequence in time to ward off her overwhelming fear response. For example, any perception of unpleasant sensations would alert her to avoid negatively escalating the next two modalities—negative thoughts and catastrophic images. In their place, she would substitute rational thinking ("I'm probably hyperventilating again. Let me do some diaphragmatic breathing."). She then would deliberately focus on pleasant and relaxing images. Someone who reported a different firing order, such as an I-C-S-A pattern (imagery-cognition-sensation-affect) would set about countervailing the anxiety quite differently.

In this *Viewer's Guide,* I have attempted to highlight certain features of the multimodal approach that underscore its comprehensive, flexible, systematic qualities, emphasizing that it is a custom-made approach to assessment and therapy. The multimodal orientation has much in common with rational–emotive–behavior therapy or cognitive–behavior therapy, but I hope that readers and viewers will discern some significant points of departure and appreciate certain features that are unique.

Dr. Lazarus identifies his approach as "multimodal therapy." What does this imply to you? More specifically, what do you expect of him? Will Dr. Lazarus be active or passive? Will the session be structured or unstructured? Directive or nondirective? Will it focus on the past or on the present? Will the session focus on behaviors, on thoughts, or on feelings? What do you expect to be the relative balance between attention to technique versus the interpersonal interaction?

Have you, or has anyone you know, undergone multimodal therapy? What was it like? Was it helpful?

Client Background and Precipitating Events

Jim

> Age: 28
> Sex: Male
> Race: Caucasian
> Marital status: Single
> Education: BA
> Occupation: Writer/waiter
> **Parents:** Father and mother are both living. Jim's father is a career military man, and according to Jim, "He runs the household

like a platoon." Jim's mother is a full-time homemaker. Jim describes her as "overworked, overtired, and harried." Jim reports that he has always tried to be a good and dutiful son and brother. "I am happiest when I am making someone else happy," he says.

Siblings: 5 older sisters, 1 younger brother. Jim was answerable to both his parents and his sisters, but he was more or less in charge of and responsible for his younger brother.

Jim decided to make an appointment with Dr. Lazarus after an upsetting event at work.

Jim is the supervisor of a crew of four waiters at a banquet house. Last week, one of the men on his crew, Todd, arrived late for a function that Jim's crew was catering. When Jim asked Todd why he was late, Todd was vague, mentioning a problem he was having with his roommate as the cause for his lateness. Jim continued to ask questions, and Todd blew up, accused Jim of prying, started knocking trays and glasses around, and then Todd stormed out. Jim was left with a three-person crew to cater the function, and the catering did not go smoothly. Some of the guests were annoyed with the poor service, and the customer who was hosting the affair complained to the manager, Jim's boss. Jim was called into the manager's office, reprimanded for having an inefficient crew, and given a warning that he would be demoted from his supervisory role if he did not shape up.

Jim was angry at his boss, angry at Todd for causing these problems, hurt that Todd had walked out, and feeling rejected and unappreciated by both his boss and Todd. Jim reports that he has been trying to help Todd for several months both at work and in his personal life by picking up the slack for him on the job and by listening to and offering solutions to his roommate problems.

After Jim's boss talked to him, Jim walked around for hours fuming and thinking, "My boss is unfair; Todd is unappreciative; I might lose my job. Why is everyone so unfair? Why am I made responsible for Todd? Can't Todd see how much I've tried to help him? I am the best crew leader, and now I might be demoted," and on and on.

This went on for hours, and Jim could not let go of these feelings. One recurring thought persisted: "This is not the first time I have felt this way."

Jim recalled a couple of previous times that he had had these feelings.

Once in college, he was working on a collaborative term paper with a study group. Jim was the group leader responsible for compiling the final product. One of the group members was not contributing his share because of problems with his girlfriend. Jim got involved in this student's problems, trying to help him out with the girl. The student thought Jim was intruding; he got angry at Jim and switched groups. The term paper was incomplete; everyone blamed Jim, and they almost failed the course. Jim was hurt, angry, and felt betrayed.

When Jim was in high school, he and his brother thought it would be a good idea for his younger brother the join the football team. Although his parents were against it, Jim convinced his parents to let his brother be on the team by promising to drive his brother to and from practice. His brother had an accident at practice; he broke his arm, and he was dropped from the team. After this, his brother was miserable. He let his school work slip, and he started cutting classes. Jim's parents were very upset about the younger boy's acting out, and they blamed Jim for the whole situation. "After all," they said, "you talked him and us into this whole football thing." Jim was very upset. He had been trying to be helpful and kind, and he was blamed for something that, as he put it, "he had nothing to do with."

What is your impression of Jim? Do you like him? How typical or atypical are his life experiences and his current behavior?

Does he need psychotherapy?

What do you believe are the core issues for Jim? What is the utility of these initial formulations?

What overall goals for therapy do you suggest?

Before you read the next section, what topics and issues do you think will be addressed in the initial sessions?

Process Notes From Initial Sessions

I briefly interviewed Jim over the telephone prior to the first appointment. Our 10-minute conversation established the presenting complaints, referral source, geographic location, and some personal and demographic data—age, marital status, occupation, and previous treatment history. Fees and insurance coverage were discussed. The telephone interview revealed no a priori reasons for referring Jim elsewhere, so an appointment was scheduled, and directions of how to get to my office were provided.

Once in the office, Jim was invited to sit in a large chair. I started with, "Let me first note down some formal details." Name, address, telephone numbers, referral source, date of meeting, and marital status were noted. The names, ages, and occupations of immediate family members were also written down. Thereafter, I said, "Well, now please tell me what brings you to me." Jim was then fairly in control of the session while I jotted down notes and made tentative inferences from my observations. Wherever appropriate, I made empathic reflections, and I sought clarification when I was unsure of particular issues or points.

By the end of the first session, in addition to understanding presenting complaints and their main precipitants, I will usually have sensed whether or not (a) psychopharmacological consultation will be necessary; (b) any signs of "psychosis" are present; (c) homicidal or suicidal intent plays any role; (d) the patient is apt to be friendly, hostile, sullen, or acquiescent; and (e) there are any tics, mannerisms, or motor disturbances. I will also determine who or what seem to be maintaining the client's maladaptive behaviors, the pace at which therapy should best proceed, and why the client is seeking therapy at this particular time.

Jim was handed the Multimodal Life History Questionnaire at the end of the first session and asked to complete it at home and bring it with him to the next session. He was also given a book that pertains to some of his specific difficulties and asked to read specific sections.

I started the second session with a general question, "How have things been going?" Soon thereafter, I addressed elements from the previous session. I glanced through the Multimodal Life History Questionnaire and asked about any significant omissions. "I see that you did not fill in some of the questions under Behavior." "You left this question blank: 'My best friend thinks I am . . .'" After a rapid reading of the material, I discussed my overall impressions and pointed out that *I* now have a homework assignment—to study the questionnaire very thoroughly and prepare a list of findings and impressions before our third session. Toward the end of the session, I summarized the main points and then discussed possible additional actions (tasks, assignments) that Jim might consider.

I reviewed the Multimodal Life History Questionnaire; drew up a Modality Profile; and noted some various specific findings, impressions and queries.

Were the initial sessions as you expected?

As you read this summary of the preceding sessions, are there any areas or topics that you think should be covered but were not? What other information would you seek to assess Jim?

Before you view the tape, what do you think will unfold in the taped session? What issues will be discussed? What will the relationship between Dr. Lazarus and Jim be like?

Viewer's Notes (Space provided for your notes.)

Stimulus Questions About the Videotaped Session

In the early part of the session, Dr. Lazarus reviews his impressions of the patient's responses to the Life History Questionnaire. This provides a structural thumbnail description of the patient's personality in terms of the BASIC I.D.

How does this enable or direct therapy? Would you be comfortable in doing this? For which patients might this prove effective?

In responding to the patient, Lazarus uses dramatic and judgmental language, such as "That's garbage!"

What are your thoughts about this?

About 8 minutes into the session: Dr. Lazarus attempts to distinguish his being critical about Jim's behavior from attacking Jim personally. Jim responds that he has been attacked his entire life and that he realizes Dr. Lazarus is pointing out his emotional and behavioral problems.

How might a therapist help the patient understand this distinction? Did you feel that this distinction was sufficiently clear? What are other ways of making this distinction?

About 13 minutes into the session: Jim recounts an emotional memory of a childhood birthday party. Dr. Lazarus responds, "This is really heavy stuff." Then he redirects Jim to consider whether this is a more general theme of his life.

What are other ways of dealing with an intense expression of feelings? Under what clinical circumstances is such a redirection away from specific memories to more general themes indicated?

About 26 minutes into the session: Following the role play, Jim offers emotionally charged childhood material, and Dr. Lazarus redirects the session to a more cognitive and contemporary focus. The patient starts, "When I was 8 . . . ." Dr. Lazarus responds, "I am more interested in . . . ." This represents a choice point, as in any session when the therapist must decide whether to stay with material as presented by the patient or refocus it.

When and under what circumstances do you do this?

Later in the session, Dr. Lazarus instructs the patient in a "time-machine technique."

How did the patient respond to this intervention? What are the advantages and disadvantages of this technique?

Dr. Lazarus further suggests that Jim role play a discussion with his father about a painful childhood incident.

How does this help Jim resolve his pain? What might be the active change process in this segment?

Reflective of his interpersonal style and his agenda for the session, Dr. Lazarus holds the Multimodal Life Questionnaire and session notes in his hand. He immediately follows up with the patient on homework and reading assignments. He came clearly prepared for the session.

What is the optimal balance for you of a therapist's being receptive to the patient initiation of material and the therapist's coming with a definite agenda?

General Questions

Did the session progress as you anticipated? Was Jim as you expected? Was Dr. Lazarus as you expected?

What are your general reactions to the session? What did you feel was effective in the therapy? What do you think were the strengths and the weaknesses of this approach?

If you were not informed that this is multimodal psychotherapy, what would you have called it? What do you think makes this distinctly multimodal?

After reading about Jim and viewing this session, what are your diagnostic impressions or characterizations of his problem?

How would you proceed with Jim's therapy? How many sessions will it take?

Therapist's Reflections on the Demonstration

Dr. Lazarus, could you share with us your impressions of and your feelings about this session?

As far as what I was doing, it's fairly consistent with what I typically do. I look for crucial areas and then try to find ways and means of eliminating the pain attached to them.

It was a good session in the sense that a number of pivotal points came out. Sometimes therapy can be pretty bland. You just chat about things and people go to sleep. I don't think that that's the case in this session. Some important issues were raised.

So, in terms of this session and its being similar to or different from your clinical work, was this was fairly representative of what you do and how you do it?

That's an interesting question. I've always said that if I was seeing a patient at ten o'clock, another at eleven, and another at twelve and if somebody watched me, not knowing me at all, the person watching me with the first patient might say, I think this must be a psychodynamic therapist. Why? Because all I was doing was listening and occasionally making some comment or tying historical events to the present. For the next patient, I was the poor man's Albert Ellis—disputing, attacking, and so on. Why was I so different? Not because I was more energetic with one patient and I was tired with the other one. No. There were valid reasons in my mind for giving the person what he or she needed. And for the next patient, I might be totally different.

As a technical eclectic, I will choose technique from many sources. I apply them without buying into the theories that spawned them. I work out of a social learning, cognitive theory. Everything I do in therapy I explain by that broad theory. But that doesn't stop me from borrowing various techniques.

I use a lot of bibliotherapy, and, for this reason, I've written a few popular books that I give patients because I find that it really expedites the therapy. It facilitates what happens. Jim mentioned in the first session that he's an avid reader, so I gave him a copy of the book. Another patient might not be a reader. But, if you gave me a different patient, a different kind of an individual, with different problems, what I would do might bear no resemblance to what I did with Jim. It might be totally different. That's why I call it "multimodal therapy."

What ideas, what themes, might you be carrying over and thinking about as you went into the next session?

Clearly, Jim had a lot of anger, pain, unresolved issues with family, and the whole question of his entitlements. I would address those points in the next session.

We would check on the relaxation to see if that works or doesn't work. I would then move into a kind of social skills training, particularly on how to deal with family members. He had said that he wanted to discuss things with his sisters, perhaps even have a little confrontation with his father. I might prepare him for that.

I would look at what's going on with the girlfriend, on the job, and see what issues crop up. We could work on social skills training in the fourth session.

Suggested Readings

Bandura, A. (1986). *Social foundations of thought and action.* Englewood Cliffs, NJ: Prentice Hall.

Dryden, W. (1991). *A dialogue with Arnold Lazarus: "It depends."* Bristol, PA: Open Universities Press.

Foa, E. B., Rothbaum, B. O., Riggs, D. S., & Murdock, T. B. (1991). Treatment of posttraumatic stress disorder in rape victims: A comparison between cognitive–behavioral procedures and counseling. *Journal of Consulting and Clinical Psychology, 59,* 715–723.

Keat, D. B. (1990). *Child multimodal therapy.* Norwood, NJ: Ablex Publishing.

Kwee, M. G. T., & Roborgh, M. R. H. M. (1987). *Multimodale therapie.* Lisse, Holland: Swets & Zeitlinger.

Lazarus, A. A. (1971). *Behavior therapy and beyond.* New York: McGraw-Hill.

Lazarus, A. A. (1976). *Multimodal behavior therapy.* New York: Springer.

Lazarus, A. A. (1989). *The practice of multimodal therapy.* Baltimore: Johns Hopkins University Press.

Lazarus, A. A. (1992a). Multimodal therapy: Technical eclecticism with minimal integration. In J. C. Norcross & M. R. Goldfried (Eds.), *Handbook of psychotherapy integration.* New York: Basic Books.

Lazarus, A. A. (1992b). The multimodal approach to the treatment of minor depression. *American Journal of Psychotherapy, 46,* 50–57.

Lazarus, A. A. (1993). Tailoring the therapeutic relationship, or being an authentic chameleon. *Psychotherapy, 30,* 404–407.

Lazarus, A. A. (1995a). Different types of eclecticism and integration: Let's be aware of the dangers. *Journal of Psychotherapy Integration, 5,* 27–39.

Lazarus, A. A. (1995b). Multimodal therapy. In R. J. Corsini & D. Wedding (Eds.), *Current psychotherapies.* Itasca, IL: Peacock.

Lazarus, A. A., & Lazarus, C. N. (1991). *Multimodal life history inventory.* Champaign, IL: Research Press.

Nelson-Jones, R. (1995). *Theory and practice of counseling.* (2nd ed.) London, England: Cassell.

Shapiro, F. (1989). Efficacy of eye-movement desensitization: A new treatment for post-traumatic stress disorder. *Journal of Behavior Therapy and Experimental Psychiatry, 20,* 211–217.

CHAPTER 9

Experiential Psychotherapy

Conducted by Alvin R. Mahrer, PhD

About Dr. Mahrer

Alvin R. Mahrer, PhD, graduated in 1954 from Ohio State University with a doctorate in clinical psychology, went to Denver to work at the VA Hospital, and became president of the Colorado Psychological Association. In 1967, he was professor and clinical director at Miami University; he later was associated with the University of Waterloo and subsequently, the University of Ottawa, where he was given the 1992 University of Ottawa Award for Excellence in Research, partly on the basis of his 10 books and approximately 180 other publications on or about psychotherapy.

What do you know about Dr. Mahrer? What are your impressions of his work from published material, conversations with and about him, or any other sources of information?

What are your expectations of Dr. Mahrer's style and behavior in conducting psychotherapy?

Synopsis of Experiential Psychotherapy

Provided by Alvin R. Mahrer, PhD

Each session is its own minitherapy because it enables the person to move in the direction of becoming a substantially new person who can be free of whatever "bad-feeling scene" was front and center in this session. Each session, including initial sessions, invites the person to go through four steps.

These four steps serve as an overall program or pattern that the therapist is to follow. However, the actual content varies with each person in just about each session, and the tempo and pace are determined by this therapist and this person working together in this session, as they proceed generally through the steps.

1. Being in a Moment of Strong Feeling: Accessing the Inner Experiencing

This step enables the person to access—be in touch with, sense—a deeper inner experiencing. Accessing a deeper potential, an inner experiencing, starts with the person's identifying some scene of strong feeling, some scene or attentional center that is accompanied by strong feelings. The feelings may be good or bad ones. Then the person is shown how to enter into this scene, to live and be in this scene. Once this scene is alive and real, the work is to discover the exact moment of strong feeling in this scene and thereby access the deeper, inner potential for experiencing. The door to the deeper, inner experiencing is the newly discovered precise moment of strong feeling in the more general scene of strong feeling. Following are the substeps for step 1:

Give opening instructions. The person is shown how to look for scenes of strong feeling, how to attend to whatever is accompanied by strong feeling.

Find a scene of strong feeling. Find a scene (time, incident, situation) in which the feeling is quite strong.

Live and be in the scene of strong feeling, and discover the precise moment of strong feeling. Enter into, live and be in, the scene of strong feeling. Search for and discover the moment, the precise instant, of strong feeling.

Access the inner experiencing. In the moment of strong feeling, access (receive, be open to, be in touch with, sense) the deeper inner experiencing.

2. Integrative Good Relationships With the Inner Experiencing

Once the inner experiencing is accessed, the second step enables the person to welcome and appreciate it, to have integrative good relationships toward it, to love and accept it, to enjoy and receive the accessed inner experiencing. It is an achievement to have integrative good relationships with what had been deeper inside the person.

The therapist and the person use a package of methods, all designed to enable the person to welcome and to appreciate the accessed inner experiencing, to feel good about this inner experiencing.

3. Being the Inner Experiencing in Earlier Scenes

This step enables the person to undergo a qualitative, radical change into "being the inner experiencing." The shift is into actually being a new person who is the inner experiencing. Being the inner experiencing is to occur within the context of scenes and situations from earlier in the person's life. Following are the substeps for step 3:

Find an earlier life scene. Find an earlier life scene by using the scene of strong feeling and accessed inner experiencing from step 1.

Be the inner experiencing in the earlier life scene. The person is to shift into being the inner experiencing in the context of the alive, real, immediate, earlier life scene.

Find other earlier life scenes, and be the inner experiencing in these other life scenes. Find other scenes throughout the person's life, scenes appropriate for being the inner experiencing. The person is to fully be the inner experiencing in these scenes.

4. Being the New Person in the Present

This step enables the person to be the qualitatively new person, in the present and prospective future, and to be free of the bad-feeling scene(s) of step 1. The inner experiencing is now an integral part of the new person, with new ways of behaving, thinking, feeling, and being, in a new world. When the session is over, the person (a) is being the new person, including the inner experiencing as a new part of the new person; (b) is ready and committed, as the new person, to being and behaving in some defined way that comes from and provides for the new inner experiencing; and (c) is relatively free, as the new person, of the bad-feeling scene(s) that was (were) front and center in step 1. Following are the substeps for step 4:

Select prospective scenes and behaviors for being the new person in playful unrealistic ways. Select extratherapy scenes from the present and from the prospective future. Select ways of being and behaving. The selected scenes and behaviors are to enable the person to be the whole new person, with emphasis on playful unreality.

Be the new person, in playfully unrealistic ways, in scenes of the present and prospective future. The patient is the new person, the inner experiencing, in scenes of the present and prospective future, and within a context of playfulness, unreality, pretense, and fantasy.

Rehearse and refine being the actual new person in present and prospective future scenes. Rehearse and refine ways of actually being the new person in the extratherapy world of the present and prospective future.

Commit to being the new person in extratherapy world. The new person is committed to the selected, rehearsed, refined new way of being and behaving in the selected extratherapy present and prospective future scenes.

Indications That the Steps Were Successful and Effective

The steps are designed to start with highly personal scenes that are accompanied by very strong feelings in order to discover the deeper potential that can be accessed from this scene; to enable the person to undergo a qualitative change into being the new person who is this pleasant, alive, inner experiencing; and to give this new person an opportunity to see what it can be like to be and behave as this wholesomely integrated and actualized new person in the present and prospective world. This momentous change includes the extinguishing of the scenes of bad feelings that were front and center in the beginning step of the session.

There are two principal ways of judging the success and effectiveness of this session. First, by the end of the session, it should be relatively clear that all four steps were attained. Because each step paves the way for the next one, the critical indication is that the fourth step has been attained with some success and effectiveness. Second, in the first step of the next session, the degree to which the person is this new person is an indication of the success and effectiveness of the previous session. If the person reverts back to essentially the same person who began the previous session, then that session was not especially successful and effective. Also, in the first step of the next session, the person should be essentially free of the bad-feeling scene(s) that was (were) front and center in the previous session. If the person has the same bad feeling in generally the same kind of scene, the previous session was not especially successful or effective.

Practical Details Related to Sessions

Telephone contact and scheduling. There are some guidelines for the telephone contact. Let the person know that you work one session at a time. At the end of each session, if you would like to have another session, and if the person is also ready and willing, then schedule the next session. You may have one or two sessions a week, for just a few sessions or for many sessions. You may have sessions over a few months or more, or for a long time, or in batches of sessions whenever the person wants. However, over the telephone, schedule this one session. Let the person know that the session ends when you both decide it is over. It may take an hour or perhaps up to two hours. Generally, sessions take $1\frac{1}{4}$ to 2 hours. Let the person know that he or she is to pay at the end of the session, and that you charge so much per hour. This is an old-fashioned way of doing business, not in keeping with most managed care systems.

The telephone contact is to be from the person who seeks the session. If a professional person or someone in the family wants to refer the person, ask the caller to tell the person being referred to give you a call so that you can make arrangements.

There is no testing, questionnaire, form, pretherapy screening, getting a case history, explanation of the therapy, or preliminary intake or interview in the telephone contact, before the first session, or in the first session. The mutual agreement is for this session alone, one session at a time.

Nor is it relevant or useful to do a screening, evaluation, assessment, or intake interview to see if the person is appropriate for experiential therapy or if experiential therapy is appropriate for this person. We do not need this (a) because we work one session at a time rather than contract for an extended series of sessions; (b) because appropriateness refers to whether or not we attain the four steps in this session; and (c) because experiential therapy is useful for any person who is ready and willing to go through the four steps in this session—this is preferable to gauging therapies in terms of a system of problems or mental disorders in which some treatments are considered more or less appropriate.

Seating arrangements. The chairs are arranged to enable both participants to put attention on whatever is of genuine concern. Accordingly, two chairs are placed alongside one another, one or two feet apart, both facing in the same direction. The chairs are high-backed, large, comfortable, with large footstools.

What the therapist and the person are to do. Throughout this session, and in every session, both the therapist and the person are to attend, as fully as possible, to whatever is front and center for the person, to the person's immediate center of attention, to the scenes and situations that are important, to whatever is "out there." This means that your eyes are closed throughout the session, and the person is invited to do the same. If you are hesitant to close your eyes throughout the session, try to attend "out there," to close your eyes occasionally, to look out there, and not to be face-to-face with the person.

Your job is first to show the person what to do and how to do it, provided the person is ready and willing. You are the relatively competent guide or teacher or instructor. Usually this means you are rather open and honest, with few if any hidden private thoughts. Your job is also to join with the person in going through the steps. This means that you are pleasantly and competently ready and willing to undergo these changes right along with the person. This also means that you are quite ready and able to feel and experience the feelings and experiences occurring in the person and to see and to live and be in the scenes that are occurring right now.

The person is the one who actually carries out what the therapist invites the person to do at each step of the session. Accordingly, just about everything depends on the person's being ready and willing to do or not to do this particular thing right now. The person's immediate degree of readiness and willingness to do this is uppermost and is to be accepted and honored, from moment to moment, throughout the session.

Being "aligned" rather than in a generally face-to-face relationship. Throughout the session, both of you are mainly attending to whatever is out there, and both of you are sharing the same feelings and experiences while essentially living and being in the same scenes. In others words, both of you are aligned, even when either one addresses the other one. This way of being with one another replaces the two of you mainly looking at, talking to, and attending to each other. Accordingly, what is ordinarily referred to as the therapist–patient relationship or helping alliance plays little or no role in this therapy.

How to start the session. Each session enables the person to go through the same four steps. Accordingly, when both are ready, the therapist shows the person how to attend to whatever is central for the person, whatever is front and center right now, whatever is accompanied by strong feelings of any kind, bad or good. The therapist shows the person how to go to the heart of the matter by seeing whatever is right here for the person, whatever the person is concerned about, worried about, compelled by, or bothered and troubled by. What is the thing that makes the person feel terrible, bad, miserable, worried, bothered, upset, awful, torn apart, rattled, confused, rotten? What are the times, the scenes, the situations, when the feelings in the person are strong, when the feelings start up, when the person is filled with strong feelings? The goal of the opening instructions is for the person to be attending mainly to strong-feeling focal centers, living and being in strong-feeling scenes, and having the accompanying strong feelings. After the initial session, the opening instructions also include the recent times and scenes consisting of the new ways of being and behaving that the person was ready and committed to carrying out at the end of the fourth step of the previous session.

Some topics that are not especially useful for our purposes. The goal is to enable the person to attain the four steps. Accordingly, it is not especially useful, and can be downright interfering, to try instead to look for what is ordinarily understood as presenting problems or diagnosed mental disorders; to get information about the person's family, schooling, childhood peer relations, or medical history; to look for what is called precipitating events or stresses; to deal with physical examinations or psychopharmacological consultations. Neither during this session nor between this and a next session is there any testing, interviewing of family members, assignment of readings, or completion of repertoires or questionnaires or inventories or checklists. Getting this kind of information is not especially useful for attaining the goals of this session.

Dr. Mahrer identifies his approach as "experiential therapy." What does this imply to you? More specifically, what do you expect of him? Will Dr. Mahrer be active or passive? Will the session be structured or unstructured? Directive or nondirective? Will it focus on the past or on the present? Will the session focus on behaviors, on thoughts, or on feelings? What do you expect to be the relative balance between attention to technique versus the interpersonal interaction?

Have you, or has anyone you know, undergone experiential therapy? What was it like? Was it helpful?

Client Background and Precipitating Events

Ted

Age: mid-thirties
Sex: Male
Race: Caucasian
Marital status: Married to Jenny
Occupation: Ted owns a fairly well-known, successful landscape business, with about 5 full-time employees and some part-time employees.
Children: Two daughters: Ann (4) and Lisa (1).
Parents: Mother and father (in good health; they also live in Ottawa).
Siblings: Two brothers: Serge (a little older than Ted) and Conrad (a little younger).

Wife: Jenny (ceramicist, fairly well known in town for her exhibits).

Ted is from a big family in Ottawa with many aunts, uncles, and cousins.

In this therapy, the session starts with an invitation for the person to put all his attention on recent times, incidents, and scenes, in which there were strong feelings. Ted had two experiences within the past week when he drove to a part of town where prostitutes are, sat in the car, thought about taking out his penis and showing it to a prostitute, but did not. He is scared by the urge.

Given this limited information, what do you believe might be the core issues for Ted?

Before you read the next section, what topics and issues do you think will be addressed in the initial sessions?

Process Notes From Initial Sessions

The opening instructions in the first session enabled Ted to live and be in two recent scenes in which he felt awful when, for the first time in his life, he drove to a part of town where there were prostitutes, sat in his car, thought about taking out his penis and showing it to a prostitute, but did not do it on either occasion. Starting from these scenes, the accessed deeper potential was described as the experiencing of being open, displaying his feelings, showing the feelings in him. By the end of the session, Ted was being this new way, and he was ready and eager to be this way with his wife especially, openly showing his feelings, including his feelings about the recent incidents with the car, the prostitutes, and his penis. I was quite drawn toward having another session, and so was Ted. We scheduled one fairly soon.

As with every session, the person has the opportunity actually to carry out the new way of being and behaving, in the context of the scene that was identified in the fourth step of the session, or perhaps in other scenes and situations between sessions in his extratherapy world.

The opening instructions in the second session enabled Ted to attend to anything that is now front and center, to any scenes of strong feeling, including scenes having to do with his "homework." His opening scenes included being this new way with his wife, and there were no further incidents involving prostitutes and bad feelings of exhibiting his penis to prostitutes from then on.

Ted moved from this scene to another one that was more central for him in this session. This scene consisted of Ted's being with his father when his father accidentally cut himself, trying to fix something, and Ted froze, felt awful, and did nothing. The accessed inner experiencing consisted of being able to be openly critical, wholesomely kidding, and playfully ridiculing. By the end of the second session, Ted was being this new person. In the fourth step of this session, Ted was ready and eager to be this new person with his father, and he rehearsed and refined being able to kid and cajole his father about something his father had done for years that no one in the family had ever mentioned openly—namely, stealing little items from stores. By the end of the second session, Ted was ready and eager to be this new way with his father and with many other people, too.

Were the initial sessions as you expected?

As you read this summary of the preceding sessions, are there any areas or topics that you think should be covered but were not? What other information would you seek to assess Ted?

Before you view the tape, what do you think will unfold in the taped session? What issues will be discussed? What will the relationship between Dr. Mahrer and Ted be like?

Viewer's Notes (Space provided for your notes.)

Stimulus Questions About the Videotaped Session

Dr. Mahrer asks Ted to close his eyes throughout the session.

What might be the various reactions that patients would have to this instruction? What might be the purpose of Dr. Mahrer's closing his eyes?

About 5 minutes into the session: Dr. Mahrer asks Ted to identify a situation or time when he experienced a strong feeling of "What's wrong with me?" Ted begins to relate a time when he was having difficulties in school, and Ted displays some anxiety regarding these memories. Dr. Mahrer quickly moves away from the memory and requests that Ted identify a more recently experienced feeling.

Under what circumstances would you follow the patient's flow of material as opposed to refocusing the course of the session? Would you have done it here? Which path would you have followed with Ted?

Dr. Mahrer persistently prompts and encourages Ted's emotional expression.

How does a therapist determine how hard to push for emotion? To what extent would you nominate specific emotions to the patient, based on your internal reactions?

About 20 minutes into the session: Ted invokes and relates a memory regarding a childhood friend whom Ted and his friends locked in a closet. Dr. Mahrer then has Ted engage in a fantasy of the memory. When complete, Dr. Mahrer states, "I can do this better than you," and he relates his own fantasy of Ted's memory. This may be construed by some patients as mutual sharing and by other patients as critical and competitive.

What are your thoughts about this exchange? How might such a therapist response enhance or impede the therapeutic process?

Dr. Mahrer uses a wide range of voice inflections and other dramatic effects during the session.

What impact do these have on Ted? On you?

Unlike most experiential therapists but similar to most cognitive–behavior therapists, Dr. Mahrer helps patients translate in-session changes to outside-session assignments.

Does this serve the same function as homework assignments in cognitive–behavior therapy? How might they differ in structure or in purpose?

Dr. Mahrer purposefully does not take a systematic clinical history of Ted.

What are the advantages and the disadvantages of not taking a formal history?

In sharing his immediate emotional experiences and physical sensations to Ted's material, Dr. Mahrer strikes many viewers as free, spontaneous, and uninhibited. This style stands in marked contrast to traditional forms of verbal psychotherapy.

For what kind of patient and problems would this approach be most effective? Least effective?

General Questions

Did the session progress as you anticipated? Was Ted as you expected? Was Dr. Mahrer as you expected?

What are your general reactions to the session? What did you feel was effective in the therapy? What do you think were the strengths and the weaknesses of this approach?

If you were not informed that this is experiential psychotherapy, what would you have called it? What do you think makes this distinctly experiential?

After reading about Ted and viewing this session, what are your diagnostic impressions or characterizations of his problem?

How would you proceed with Ted's therapy? How many sessions will it take?

Therapist's Reflections on the Demonstration

Dr. Mahrer, what were your impressions of this demonstration?

I'm reasonably satisfied that we went through the four steps that I go through. Usually I have more feeling. I'm really living in the scenes—really being there with Jenny. I was only 20 to 30% in the scene.

How was this demonstration typical of your clinical work, and were there ways in which it was atypical or unrepresentative?

Typically, every session flows through the four steps. Essentially, we start by trying to "live" or "be in" some scene, find some strong feeling, and open up something deeper. Second, we want to feel good about whatever we opened up. Third, let the patient be whatever we open up in the context of earlier scenes. Finally, and most important, is that the patient be able to be this kind of new person, out in the real world, not having the kind of bad feelings that he first brought up. Those are the four steps I want to achieve. We went through them. That's typical.

On the basis of this session, is there anything in particular that you are going to be carrying over for the next session? Are there any particular things that you want the patient to carry over?

I'll start the next session by giving Ted the same invitation to look out there, look for times, scenes, or incidents where he's had some strong feelings, good or bad, and I'll include a few possibilities for him.

"Did you really have a great feeling of being loving and enfolding with Jenny and with your father-in-law?" "And are you really free now—free of having bad feelings?" I'll carry this over in the beginning of the next session.

You were saying that you felt that you were only 20 or 30% in this session, that you were not really "living in the scenes." Do you mean that you were not feeling them, or were you were having trouble getting the image of them—or perhaps both?

Both. Usually I would see Jenny so vividly that she would be real, right in front of me. That's one thing. And the feelings that go along with what Ted is saying would be so real that there would be tears. It has to be so real and so alive that it's as if I'm just bursting with love and caring for Jenny who's really right here. I wasn't able to do that. I was too tight, scared, nervous, and I pulled away. I usually am 90, 95, almost a 100% "there," throughout the whole session.

Everything I do in the session is literally to put me in the scenes that Ted is describing. When he mentions Jake, I see Jake. My aim is for me to live literally in that scene with Ted and whoever Jake is. If Ted mentions Jake, and I "see" a big guy, I'll say, "Is he a big guy? He's a real big guy, I can see him." When Ted says, "No, he's a little boy. He's a little boy who kind of has a funny look on his face," I'll shift to what Ted's seeing. I'm always seeing things through the words that he's saying. He's creating these scenes for me.

There are times when it seemed that you wanted Ted to speak more to describe the scene in greater detail. How many sessions does it usually take for the patient and you to be spontaneous and in that image?

The critical factor is me. If I am tense, nervous, distant, then it may take me a long time, a whole session before I get into the scene. But, if I feel all right, then with just about any patient, we go right to it in the first session. I find that just about every patient, with almost no exception, can go through these steps really well—especially since we have our eyes closed and we're not looking at each other. If I'm ready, it happens with every patient at the beginning of the first session and continues.

You are saying very clearly that you guide, facilitate, and help make it happen and that your experience is that, when you are ready, almost every patient almost all the time is able to get into the experience.

Right. If a patient says, "I don't think I want to do this", I say, "Okay." We stop instantly. But, if they are ready, we can go through a session delightfully if I'm good. If I'm totally plugged in, I really see what's going on out there.

Suggested Readings

Binswanger, L. (1967). *Being-in-the-world.* New York: Harper.

Mahrer, A. R. (1986). *Therapeutic experiencing: The process of change.* New York: Norton.

Mahrer, A. R. (1989a). *Experiencing: A humanistic theory of psychology and psychiatry.* Ottawa: University of Ottawa Press.

Mahrer, A.R. (1989b). *Experiential psychotherapy: Basic practices.* Ottawa: University of Ottawa Press.

Mahrer, A. R. (1989c). *Dream work in psychotherapy and self-change.* New York: Norton.

Mahrer, A. R. (1989d). *How to do experiential psychotherapy: A manual for practitioners.* Ottawa: University of Ottawa Press.

Mahrer, A. R. (1989e). *The integration of psychotherapies: A guide for practicing therapists.* New York: Human Sciences.

Mahrer, A. R. (1990). Experiential psychotherapy. In J. K. Zeig & W. M. Munion (Eds.), *What is psychotherapy? Contemporary perspectives* (pp. 92–96). San Francisco: Jossey-Bass.

Mahrer, A. R. (1995). *The complete handbook of experiential psychotherapy.* New York: Wiley.

Mahrer, A. R., Boulet, D. B., & Fairweather, D. R. (1994). Beyond empathy: Advances in the clinical theory and methods of empathy. *Clinical Psychology Review, 14,* 183–198.

Mahrer, A. R., & Fairweather, D. R. (1993). What is experiencing? A critical review of meanings and applications in psychotherapy. *The Humanistic Psychologist, 21,* 2–25.

Mahrer, A. R., & Roberge, M. (1993). Single-session experiential therapy with any person whatsoever. In R. A. Wells & V. J. Giannetti (Eds.), *Casebook of the brief therapies.* (pp. 179–196). New York: Plenum.

May, R., Angel, E., & Ellenberger, H. F. (Eds.). (1958). *Existence: A new dimension in psychiatry and psychology.* New York: Basic Books.

Prescriptive Eclectic Therapy

Conducted by John C. Norcross, PhD

About Dr. Norcross

John C. Norcross, PhD, earned his doctorate in clinical psychology at the University of Rhode Island and completed his internship at the Brown University School of Medicine. He is professor and former chair of psychology at the University of Scranton, a clinical psychologist in part-time independent practice, and an authority on psychotherapy integration and prescriptive treatments. Author of more than 100 scholarly articles, Dr. Norcross has written or edited 10 books, including the third edition of *Systems of Psychotherapy: A Transtheoretical Analysis* (with Prochaska, 1994), *Handbook of Psychotherapy Integration* (with Goldfried, 1992) and *An Insider's Guide to Graduate Programs in Clinical Psychology* (with Mayne and Sayette, 1994). He has served on the editorial board of 10 journals and received numerous awards for his research and teaching. With his wife, two children, and weimaraner, he works and plays in the northern Pocono Mountains.

What do you know about Dr. Norcross? What are your impressions of his work from published material, conversations with and about him, or any other sources of information?

What are your expectations of Dr. Norcross' style and behavior in conducting psychotherapy?

Synopsis of Prescriptive Eclectic Therapy
Provided by John C. Norcross, PhD

This psychotherapy attempts to customize psychological treatments and therapeutic relationships to the specific needs of individual patients. It does so by drawing on effective methods from across theoretical camps (eclecticism) and by matching those methods to particular cases on the basis of empirically supported guidelines (prescriptionism). The end result of prescriptive matching is a more efficient, applicable, and efficacious therapy that fits both the client and the clinician.

Three cardinal features of prescriptive eclecticism are the synergy of awareness and action, the complementary nature of psychotherapy systems, and the identification of empirical markers for selecting psychological therapies. Awareness and action are reciprocally facilitative endeavors: Awareness informs and fuels concrete actions, and action propels and deepens meaningful insights. Hence, both awareness-oriented and action-oriented methods are indicated for most patients.

Correspondingly, the ostensibly contradictory systems of psychotherapy are seen not as contradictory but as complementary. Psychodynamic, behavioral, systemic, experiential, cognitive, and interpersonal traditions can be profitably integrated into one psychotherapy case or into one psychotherapy session in ways that maximize their respective domains of expertise.

All empirically supported systems of psychotherapy have a place, then, in the repertoire of the eclectic therapist—that place being determined by prescriptive guidelines. Prescriptive guidelines are based on controlled outcome research and clinical experience, in contrast to theoretical predilection or institutional custom, and are applied to both treatment methods *and* relationships stances. For determining the "psychotherapy of choice," these guidelines would include the disorders, treatment goals, motivational arousal, and the stages of change. For selecting the "therapeutic relationship of choice," the guidelines include patient expectancies, reactance level, and the anaclitic/sociotropy–introjective/autonomy continuum.

Prescriptive eclectic therapy transcends the "dogma eat dogma" ambience that has historically hindered advances in psychotherapy and offers an integrative structure for customizing the therapeutic enterprise. The therapy is not yet another "school" of psychotherapy, but rather an open system that attempts to incorporate the clinical research and wisdom of many clinicians, particularly that of Beutler, Lazarus, Prochaska, and DiClemente (see Suggested Readings). The prescriptive eclectic will be flexible but systematic, creative and yet empirical, in tailoring psychotherapy to the individual in his or her singular situation.

Dr. Norcross identifies his approach as "prescriptive eclectic therapy." What does this imply to you? More specifically, what do you expect of him? Will Dr. Norcross be active or passive? Will the session be structured or unstructured? Directive or nondirective? Will it focus on the past or on the present? Will the session focus on behaviors, on thoughts, or on feelings? What do you expect to be the relative balance between attention to technique versus the interpersonal interaction?

Have you, or has anyone you know, undergone eclectic or integrative therapy? What was it like? Was it helpful?

Client Background and Precipitating Events

Sam

Age: 32
Sex: Male
Race: Caucasian
Marital status: Divorced 3 years ago (married a total of 4 years)
Education: MA
Occupation: Sound engineer
Parents: Sam's parents died in an auto accident when Sam was 12. After his parents' death, Sam and his younger sister were was raised by a maternal aunt and uncle. Although Sam remembers his parents of origin, he views his aunt and uncle as his parents.

Siblings: 1 younger sister; 3 male cousins whom Sam views as brothers.

Sam is a sound engineer at a network radio station. Two weeks ago, he had a 7:00 a.m. appointment to do a voice-over for a spot that was to break on the 8:00 morning show the same day.

The night before this appointment, Sam stopped at his neighborhood bar on his way home from work to have a few drinks. Janice, his live-in companion for the last 9 months, was away on business, so he figured he would stop and pick up a sandwich after leaving the bar, go home, eat, and go to bed.

When he got to the bar, things were lively. After a couple of drinks, Sam was ready to leave, when Dave, a friend, came in. Sam ordered a round for Dave, the woman Sam had been talking with, and himself. They talked about work, about people, and so on for a hour or so, when Dave suggested that they go to Dave's house, just a couple of blocks away, to snort a few lines of cocaine. At this point, Sam was feeling good and thought, "What the hell." Sam, Lucy (the woman), and Dave headed over to Dave's place. At Dave's, they had some more drinks, listened to tapes, and did about $\frac{1}{2}$ gram of cocaine among the three of them. By this time, it was about 1:30 a.m., and Sam was really "on a roll." When Dave went to the corner deli to get some ice, Sam asked Lucy if she wanted to go back to his place. She said yes, so when Dave returned, they had another short drink and left.

When the phone rang at 7:10 a.m., Sam was a wreck. He and Lucy were on the couch in his living room, their clothes all over the place, music blaring. He felt sick and his head was throbbing. The station was calling to find out "where the hell he was!" Sam told Lucy she had better gather her things and leave. He dragged himself into the shower, threw on some clothes, and took a taxi downtown to the station. When he walked in the sound studio, it was 8:45. They had missed the spot; the talent had to be paid anyway, the producer was fuming, and Sam "felt like hell." In the back of his mind, he hoped that Lucy had gotten all her things when she left because Janice was due home before him at 3:30 today.

What was he doing? He had ruined a very lucrative spot. Why had he drunk so much? He always had a couple of drinks, but this was "weekend" style, and it was only Wednesday. Why had he done coke again on a weeknight? Lucy had been right for the moment, but what if Janice had come home early and "found" him? What if the place had signs of Lucy when Janice got home at 3:30 today? He felt miserable, and for the first time, he was scared about the way his life was going.

About 3 months ago, Sam went out with some clients after a day in the studio. They went to the clients' hotel room, did a gram of coke, and drank a lot of Scotch. Sam wound up staying out all night. He went into work the next day with no sleep, just getting by on coffee and cigarettes. He did not remember much of what he had said or done. When the clients took their next job to another station, Sam wondered if he had committed social and professional suicide.

Toward the end of his marriage, Sam was drinking a lot, and he and his wife were constantly fighting. He occasionally "fooled around" with other women, never going to bed with anyone more than two or three times. The women never really meant much to him. He was just bored—with his wife, his life, everything. Right before the final breakup with his wife, one of the women from his office, with whom he had slept on and off for about 3 months, called his wife and told her about Sam's liaisons with different women at work. His wife said she had had it, and she left for good. Sam was depressed, but he thought that it was for the best. Maybe now he would have some peace and quiet. Maybe now that she was gone he would not drink so much.

What is your impression of Sam? Do you like him? How typical or atypical are his life experiences and his current behavior?

Does he need psychotherapy?

What do you believe are the core issues for Sam? What is the utility of these initial formulations?

What overall goals for therapy do you suggest?

Before you read the next section, what topics and issues do you think will be addressed in the initial sessions?

Process Notes From Initial Sessions

On the referral of a friend, Sam telephoned our office to request an appointment with me. The office manager collected basic demographic information, explained office procedures and fee arrangements, and gave Sam the first available appointment, 2 weeks from then.

I began the initial interview with the standard questions, "What brings you here at this time in your life?" and "How can I help?" Sam proceeded to relate the recent disturbing patterns in his life, accompanied by a display of substantial emotion. I followed Sam's lead, listening attentively, offering empathy, and occasionally requesting clarification.

After Sam had related his story, I briefly ascertained the relevant clinical, psychiatric, and medical histories. I asked Sam to complete a Life History Questionnaire and a computerized Minnesota Multiphasic Personality Inventory–2 (MMPI-2) prior to our next interview, in the interest of efficiently obtaining comprehensive biographical and psychological information. Sam readily agreed.

Thereafter, I described my way of working. The first two sessions are largely for gathering information, developing rapport, and determining whether there is a "good enough match" between patient and therapist; the third session begins psychotherapy proper. I emphasized the importance of a collaborative relationship in determining the process and goals of therapy and shared specific examples from our initial 40 minutes together. I suggested that, within an empathic and empowering relationship, we tentatively move toward both awareness of Sam's problems and their origins as well as concrete actions to resolve them. Sam immediately concurred, saying, "I want to understand myself and also get myself out of this downward spiral." We agreed to use mutually created between-session tasks (or homework assignments). I proposed that an immediate start in this direction would be for Sam to remain abstinent from alcohol and other drugs for a least a month. Sam agreed.

At the close of the first, 60-minute interview, I asked Sam what questions he might have of me and my way of working. Sam asked three questions. The first concerned my position at the local university, which I answered in a factual manner. The second question was, "What should I call you?" I asked Sam what he would be most comfortable with; Sam responded, "John, if that's OK," to which I responded, "That works for me. May I call you Sam?" Sam nodded in the affirmative. Sam's third question was, "Do you think you can help me?" I immediately reflected that Sam might be feeling afraid and uncertain about psychotherapy, and Sam responded, "Yeah, it's kinda scary," adding, "I've never done this (psychotherapy) before." I stated that I sincerely believed that psychotherapy could help Sam, "providing that we work hard together." The session ended with my asking Sam to consider whether I was the right therapist for him and reminding him to please complete the questionnaire and psychological testing prior to our next session.

Before the second session, Sam completed the Life History Questionnaire and a computer-administered MMPI-2.

In the second session, I welcomed Sam and, within a minute or two, inquired how Sam experienced the first session. Sam replied that "it went well" and noted that he had been "less upset" over the past week. I then wondered aloud whether Sam thought we were a "good enough match" to work together. Sam stated, "Yes, I feel comfortable with you and what we spoke about." I stated that I, too, felt positive about our first meeting and that I was impressed with Sam's candor and commitment, particularly since this was Sam's first experience with psychotherapy.

The remainder of the session was devoted to completing the clinical assessment, strengthening the therapeutic alliance, and setting the stage for psychotherapy in ensuing sessions. Together, we reviewed the results of the Life History Questionnaire, especially an eerie convergence of Sam's own problems and those of his biological father, and of the MMPI-2, which indicated moderate depression, substance abuse, and medium-to-high resistance to external controlling influence. We then constructed a multigenerational genogram as a structured device to elicit family and social-developmental histories.

In an effort to begin tailoring the psychotherapy specifically to Sam's needs, I asked a series of questions about Sam's expectations, stage of change, and interpersonal style. Sam reported that he benefited most from a fairly active, informal, and active therapeutic relationship—"someone who cares but who kicks me in the butt if I need it." He also confirmed the testing results that he did not like to be externally controlled "unless I'm a big part of the decision."

Toward the conclusion of the session, Sam agreed that depression, boredom, "infidelity," and a slow descent into self-destruction were problems he would like to confront (action stage). However, he was uncertain whether drugs and alcohol constituted a serious problem (no denial but some minimization; contemplation stage). He declined a referral to Alcoholics Anonymous or Rational Recovery, "at least not now." He did agree to remain abstinent for another month (for a total of 2 months) to determine how alcohol and cocaine abuse affects his mood. We contracted for weekly individual psychotherapy sessions, combining both awareness and action strategies, including between-session tasks. The mutually defined tasks during the next week were for Sam to obtain a thorough medical evaluation, to remain abstinent, and to reflect on the striking parallels between his current problems and those of his father.

Were the initial sessions as you expected?

As you read this summary of the preceding sessions, are there any areas or topics that you think should be covered but were not? What other information would you seek to assess Sam?

Before you view the tape, what do you think will unfold in the taped session? What issues will be discussed? What will the relationship between Dr. Norcross and Sam be like?

Viewer's Notes (Space provided for your notes.)

Stimulus Questions About the Videotaped Session

Dr. Norcross opens with the greeting, "Well, Sam, it's good to see you again." Dr. Norcross then notes that they are in their third session together and invites Sam's comments on the therapist and the therapy.

How and in what way is their opening different from and similar to the openings of sessions by other therapists?

About 8 minutes into the session: Dr. Norcross comments on the empirical data to support the palliative effects of exercise on depression.

Did you feel that this use of supportive research findings seemed to flow naturally in the exchange? When have you used research data in the course of psychotherapy?

About 11 minutes into the session: Responding to Sam's discomfort with the homework assignment of thinking about the parallel between Sam's father's behavior and Sam's own behavior, Dr. Norcross attempts to guide Sam toward a greater exploration and awareness of his feelings with neutral statements such as, "How should we proceed?" "Should we spend more time on this?" and "Let's go slowly."

With these neutral statements, is Dr. Norcross working on the content of Sam's thoughts or the patient–therapist relationship?

About 17 minutes into the session: Sam talks about the loss of his parents. Dr. Norcross notes Sam's sadness with the comment, "Your voice is getting a little moist." Dr. Norcross gently coaxes further thinking with comments that it was sudden and painful and that it "wasn't grieved and resolved." As the emotion increased, Sam says, " Haven't I already told you this," and Dr. Norcross makes the comment, "Just the facts, so to speak." Sam is clearly feeling, and showing, discomfort about discussing the loss of his parents, and Dr. Norcross' interventions highlight the distressful feelings and the loss.

What do you make of it? Under what conditions would you, as a therapist, work to intensify or lessen the experience of distressful emotion in therapy?

About 22 minutes into the session: After 10 minutes of intense discussion, Sam stops talking. Dr. Norcross pushes and prods further, attempting to get Sam to continue. Dr. Norcross then talks for about 2 minutes about the value of talking about emotionally laden issues in therapy and ends by describing the importance of "dosing" the amount of stress and anxiety experienced in therapy.

How is Dr. Norcross' behavior similar or dissimilar from his earlier interventions? What do you feel is gained—or lost—by this action at this moment in therapy?

About 30 minutes into the session: After a noticeable 20-second pause, Dr. Norcross asks, "What are you experiencing right now? What are you feeling?"

How did you feel during the silence? Would you have broken the silence? If so, how would you have done it?

Dr. Norcross' style involves instruction and reassurance, requests for permission to approach issues, careful approach to subjects, and summarizing and using terms such as "doses" of discussion.

How does this approach and personal style enhance the therapeutic alliance?

General Questions

Did the session progress as you anticipated? Was Sam as you expected? Was Dr. Norcross as you expected?

What are your general reactions to the session? What did you feel was effective in the therapy? What do you think were the strengths and the weaknesses of this approach?

If you were not informed that this is prescriptive eclectic psychotherapy, what would you have called it? What do you think makes this distinctly prescriptive eclectic?

After reading about Sam and viewing this session, what are your diagnostic impressions or characterizations of his problem?

How would you proceed with Sam's therapy? How many sessions will it take?

Therapist's Reflections on the Demonstration

Dr. Norcross, what were your impressions and your feelings about the session?

I think I was largely able to succeed in securing the three goals I have for an early session in an ongoing course of psychological treatment. The first goal is to make an empathic connection, to forge a therapeutic alliance. Second, I tried to establish continuity between the first two sessions, which were largely evaluation sessions, and this session, in which I am doing therapy. Third, I want to make the therapy begin. We've gone through some of the prerequisites and preparatory stages, and now we're getting to it. We need to mutually develop a path and a direction.

How representative was this demonstration of your therapy as you usually do it? What are the things that are atypical?

It was representative in terms of the types of patients I see. I see patients suffering from depression, drug and alcohol abuse, infidelity and affairs, and a sense of meaninglessness or alienation.

In terms of the therapy process itself, it is more difficult to say how typical it was of my work. We try to individualize, tailor each session for each new patient. Nonetheless, some things do stick out in my mind as fairly typical of me. I reflect on the session as a combination of types of intervention—some supportive, some directive, some exploratory. In cases with a man like Sam, when one might suspect drugs and alcohol dependency, I usually do request a period of abstinence. Also, if someone hasn't had a thorough physical examination in a while, I probably suggest that as well.

What's not typical about the session is that in most cases with a client like Sam, by the fourth or fifth session, I typically request that a significant other come in at least for one session to ascertain her perspective, to elicit her support for treatment and see how they interact.

On the basis of this session, what might you be carrying over, what might you be thinking of during the week between sessions?

I wonder how Sam is experiencing these therapy sessions. Are we going too fast or too slow? I emphasized that he set the pace here as long as he continues to address painful topics. I'll come back into the next session thinking, How is he experiencing being in treatment?

Something else that strikes me—lurking in the back of my mind—is, because this man is suffering from depression and from alcohol and drug abuse, how's he doing here? I don't think he's going to require a formal rehabilitation program or an antidepressant, but they remain active possibilities, depending on his response to treatment.

And last, I think what I would carry over is to work to keep the therapy moving.

Suggested Readings

Beutler, L. E., & Clarkin, J. F. (1990). *Systematic treatment selection.* New York: Brunner/Mazel.

Dryden, W. (1991). *A dialogue with John Norcross: Toward integration.* London: Open University Press.

Feldman, L. B. (1992). *Integrating individual and family therapy.* New York: Brunner/Mazel.

Lazarus, A. A. (1989). *The practice of multimodal therapy.* Baltimore: Johns Hopkins University Press.

Lazarus, A. A., Beutler, L. E., & Norcross, J. C. (1992). The future of technical eclecticism. *Psychotherapy, 29,* 11–20.

Norcross, J. C. (Ed.). (1987). *Casebook of eclectic psychotherapy.* New York: Brunner/Mazel.

Norcross, J. C. (1991). (Special section editor). Prescriptive matching in psychotherapy: Psychoanalysis for simple phobias? *Psychotherapy, 28,* 439–472.

Norcross, J. C. (1993). The relationship of choice: Matching the therapist's stance to individual clients. *Psychotherapy, 30,* 402–413.

Norcross, J. C., & Goldfried, M. R. (Eds.). (1992). *Handbook of psychotherapy integration.* New York: Basic Books.

Prochaska, J. O., DiClemente, C. C., & Norcross, J. C. (1992). In search of how people change: Applications to addictive behaviors. *American Psychologist, 47,* 1102–1114.

Prochaska, J. O., & Norcross, J. C. (1994). *Systems of psychotherapy: A transtheoretical analysis* (3rd ed.). Pacific Grove, CA: Brooks/Cole.

Prochaska, J. O., Norcross, J. C., & DiClemente, C. C. (1994). *Changing for good.* New York: William Morrow.

Saltzman, N., & Norcross, J. C. (Eds.). (1990). *Therapy wars: Contention and convergence in differing clinical approaches.* San Francisco: Jossey-Bass.

CHAPTER 11

Cognitive–Behavior Therapy

Conducted by Jacqueline B. Persons, PhD

About Dr. Persons

Jacqueline B. Persons, PhD, received her undergraduate degree in anthropology from the University of Chicago in 1972 and her PhD in clinical psychology from the University of Pennsylvania in 1979. Dr. Persons is a clinician, researcher, teacher, and writer. She has a private practice in Oakland, CA, and is associate clinical professor in the Department of Psychiatry, University of California, San Francisco, where she provides clinical and research training to pre- and postdoctoral psychologists and to psychiatric residents. She is the author of *Cognitive Therapy in Practice: A Case Formulation Approach* (1989; translated into Japanese in 1993).

What do you know about Dr. Persons? What are your impressions of her work from published material, conversations with and about her, or any other sources of information?

What are your expectations of Dr. Persons' style and behavior in conducting psychotherapy?

Synopsis of Cognitive–Behavior Therapy

Provided by Jacqueline B. Persons, PhD

Following are descriptions of central features of cognitive–behavior therapy (CBT).

A Primary Therapeutic Goal of Solving Overt Problems and Reducing Symptoms

Although cognitive–behavior (CB) therapists do focus on underlying mechanisms that are proposed to cause overt problems (e.g., a view of the self as inadequate that contributes to symptoms of anxiety), the primary goal of cognitive–behavior therapy is to alleviate the overt problems. As part of the emphasis on solving overt problems, CB therapists attempt to measure those problems in concrete, objective terms so that the outcome of the therapy can be assessed. The therapy cannot be considered successful if overt problems and symptoms do not change. However, the cognitive–behavioral model does view underlying mechanisms (e.g., schemas) as causal in activating symptoms and therefore proposes that if symptoms are solved and underlying mechanisms remain intact, the patient is vulnerable to relapse. Thus, changing underlying mechanisms is a goal of CBT, but a secondary one.

The CB therapist adopts a "top down" view of change, proposing that changes in symptoms and behaviors (e.g., increased exposure to feared situations, with decreased anxiety in those situations) feed "downward" to underlying mechanisms and result in schema change ("I handled that question effectively; maybe I'm not so inadequate after all.").

An Empirical Attitude

CB therapists have been leaders in the objective study of the outcome of clinical interventions. Thus, a large outcome literature exists regarding CB therapies, which demonstrates their effectiveness in the treatment of a host of clinical disorders and problems, including clinical depression; anxiety disorders (including the social phobia illustrated in the videotape therapy session); eating disorders; couples problems; substance abuse; irritable bowel syndrome; and many other problems in the arena of behavioral medicine, disorders of childhood, and the social skills deficits of schizophrenics.

The CB therapist strives to use methods in his or her practice that have been shown to be effective in controlled studies. Of course, this is difficult to do, as controlled studies demonstrate efficacy for an average patient, usually from a homogeneous sample of relatively simple cases, and do not say anything about the interventions likely to be helpful for the patient in the clinician's office at any particular moment.

To address this issue, the CB therapist adopts an empirical attitude to the treatment of each individual case, collecting data in an ongoing way (e.g., measuring depressive symptoms weekly, using the Beck Depression Inventory) to monitor treatment outcome. The case conceptualization (discussed later) is the hypothesis that the therapist uses to derive interventions, and the patient's response to the interventions can be seen as a measure of the accuracy of the formulation.

An Active, Structured, Problem-Solving Approach

The stance of the CB therapist is to actively seek solutions to the patient's problems. The typical CBT session is structured and goal-directed. At the beginning of the session, patient and therapist set an agenda, and at the end of the session, they review what was accomplished. In a typical CB session, patient and therapist focus on a specific problem and work together to solve it. Not infrequently, however, a key "solution" strategy involves working to increase the patient's acceptance of a problem, feeling, or situation.

A Focus on the Present

Sessions of CBT generally involve a discussion of current (or even future) situations and events. There are several exceptions, of course. Past upsetting situations, including very early ones, can be tackled in CBT. In fact, exposure methods are often used; systematic work to decondition a patient's reaction to a past trauma might involve repeatedly reviewing and reactivating the trauma until the emotional upset it arouses has been overcome. The CB therapist would generally do this, however, only when there is clear evidence that the past trauma is causing difficulties in the patient's current functioning. The CB therapist also collects a good family and social history; this information is important for several reasons, particularly in developing a useful case conceptualization.

A Collaborative Patient–Therapist Relationship

The CB therapist's stance is, "Let's work together to solve problems." The CB therapist strives to develop a collaborative patient–therapist relationship in which the therapist is not seen as "knowing all the answers," but plays the role of consultant working to help the patient find the solutions that are most helpful to him or her. Of course, some patients, because of their psychopathology, have difficulty developing or accepting a collaborative working relationship with the therapist. They may be suspicious, have difficulty trusting, or insist on idealizing the therapist and seeing him or her as the repository of all knowledge and happiness. When this happens, the CB therapist must accommodate; one strategy that might help the CB therapist do this is to reframe an increase in the collaborative nature of the patient–therapist relationship as a goal rather than a prerequisite of the therapy. In addition, of course, the CB therapist can use the nature of the patient–therapist interactions as a source of information about the patient's difficulties and as a way of doing some in vivo work on them.

Use of an Individualized Case Conceptualization

A case formulation is a case-specific "theory" that the CB therapist uses to understand the patients' problems and the relationships among them and to guide interventions, facilitate the development of a collaborative patient–therapist relationship, and understand noncompliance. As case formulation might offer a conceptualization that is stated in schema terms (e.g., in propositions about the patient's views of self, others, and the world), or in functional terms, as in traditional behavioral analysis. A case-specific formulation is particularly useful when working with patients who have multiple problems and thus cannot be easily treated with a single standardized protocol.

Reliance on Cognitive and Learning Theories

CB therapists rely on an ever-expanding set of theories of behavior and cognition, including Beck's cognitive theory of depression, Lewinson's cognitive–behavioral theory, Seligman and Johnston's cognitive view of avoidance learning, and Foa and Kozak's cognitive model of the effectiveness of behavioral exposure treatments. These models view clinical problems as understandable using a framework of mutually reciprocally connected behaviors, cognitions, and affects, activated by environmental events. These models are stated in empirically testable terms. They can be used by CB therapists to derive new interventions to address unique clinical situations.

Homework

The key role of homework in CBT draws directly on the view of therapy as a place where the patient learns new skills. New skills, to be developed and to become automatic, must be practiced. Several studies show that patients who do homework improve more than patients who do not, although more research on this is needed.

The importance of homework in CBT is also related to the key role that experiencing plays in successful therapy. CBT can seem like an intellectual, emotionally sterile approach, where patients and therapists engage in intellectual debates as to whether human beings are or are not fundamentally worthwhile. Intellectual discussions rarely (in my view) produce important clinical change. New experiences do. New experiences frequently happen in therapy sessions (e.g., the patient describes problems and the therapist is not critical, abusive, or rejecting). The purpose of homework assignments is to increase the frequency of new experiences (e.g., the patient rides in the elevator in his office building and does not have a panic attack and die).

Dr. Persons identifies her approach as "cognitive–behavior therapy." What does this imply to you? More specifically, what do you expect of her? Will Dr. Persons be active or passive? Will the session be structured or unstructured? Directive or nondirective? Will it focus on the past or on the present? Will the session focus on behaviors, on thoughts, or on feelings? What do you expect to be the relative balance between attention to technique versus the interpersonal interaction?

Have you, or has anyone you know, undergone cognitive–behavior therapy? What was it like? Was it helpful?

Client Background and Precipitating Events

Lisa

Age: 29
Sex: Female
Race: Caucasian
Marital status: Single
Education: MA, Public Relations
Occupation: Public relations manager
Parents: Father (60, BS, engineer); mother (58, BA, full-time homemaker).
Siblings: One older sister.

From the earliest ages, the father has been very involved with his daughters. He taught them to read, to swim, to try out for cheerleading, anything that involved learning new skills and strategies to succeed. He trained his daughters to carefully analyze and plan in all situations. Lisa remembers him saying, over and over, "Think it through, plan it out, and you'll win." He taught his daughters that they could achieve anything they wanted if they worked hard at it.

Lisa feels that her mother has always been critical of both of her daughters—quick to point out what they do not do right.

The sisters have always had a warm and close relationship. They have a healthy competition between them.

Lisa went to see a physician at her health maintenance organization (HMO) complaining of dizziness and fainting spells about a month ago. Lisa made an appointment to see Dr. Persons based on a referral from her HMO, commenting on a growing sense of avoiding the more "social" events at work.

About 5 weeks ago, Lisa attended the annual San Francisco Bay area awards banquet of the Public Relations Society of America. Lisa's boss, Andrea, is the president of the local chapter of the Public Relations Society of America and was going to be the "mistress of ceremonies" at the banquet. Andrea was to give a few opening remarks, introduce the speakers, announce the award winners, and make the closing remarks.

As Lisa entered the awards banquet, Andrea's administrative assistant ran up to her in the lobby of the hotel, completely flustered and obviously upset. Andrea had been in a minor car accident on the way to the banquet. Andrea had called from the hospital emergency room to tell Lisa that she would have to "fill in for her and just wing it as the mistress of ceremonies" for the evening. When Lisa heard this, she thought she "was going to be sick." "Not the part about Andrea's accident," she told Dr. Persons, "but that I would have to be on stage as the mistress of ceremonies and make it all happen without being prepared." Lisa "knew that she couldn't get out of this." But her initial reaction was to "run out the door." "I can't do this," she thought. "Nobody has briefed me. I didn't wear the right clothes for this role. *Oh my God*, what am I going to do?" Lisa felt that her job would be on the line if she did not "pull this off," so she went to the ladies' rest room, washed her face with cool water, retouched her makeup, and went back out to the banquet room. As Lisa told Dr. Persons, "I felt the room closing in as I walked toward the podium; I felt like I couldn't breathe, and I couldn't hear anything around me, but I kept thinking 'Stay cool.'" Lisa told Dr. Persons that she was "using every ounce of strength I had to walk up the steps of the stage and take the microphone in front of all of those people." The next thing Lisa remembers is "lying on a cot in some back room and having a group of people hovering over me, asking me if I was OK." Lisa had fainted on stage and had been carried backstage.

Lisa has always been very good at her job, and she prides herself on how rapidly she has ascended in her firm. About 6 months ago, she received a monetary award and public praise before the board of directors for the most successful presentation of a new product. Andrea also nominated her campaign for the next award of the local chapter of the Public Relations Society of America. Lisa had worked for weeks on the release of this product: She had all of the background material on competing products; she had completely researched the market; she knew the target audience for the product; she worked with the marketing staff to prepare a "sophisticated, subtle, and highly effective" promotional strategy. As Lisa put it, "I knew this product and its potential, inside out." And this was not the first time that Lisa had orchestrated and executed the public relations around a highly visible and successful project. Lisa knew she was "damn good at her job!"

But then there were times when she felt anxious and uncomfortable in certain work situations. Over the past year, Lisa recalled several times when she felt dizzy and faint and as if she just wanted to run away. At these times, Lisa told Dr. Persons that she had to use "all her concentration to remain calm and in control." However, she knows that she is now frequently trying to avoid certain work situations, such as unexpected meetings with new clients and emergency meetings on suddenly emerging corporate problems. One such incident was about 4 months ago.

Lisa learned at 3:00 p.m. that the *Wall Street Journal* would be breaking a negative story the next day on one of the company's new products. She knew little about the product and had not been involved in its initial promotion. She began to feel nervous as she heard rumors about the *Journal* story and a late afternoon meeting about it. She left for the gym, as "it isn't my product." When she returned, she was pulled into the meeting, which was half over. To her surprise, she was assigned to handle the situation. Lisa had overnight to prepare a press release, brief the chief engineer for the conference, and prepare her own remarks as the chief spokesperson for her company. Lisa was "beside herself." She recalls feeling that she wanted to "just flee the scene, to jump ship." Lisa told Dr. Persons, "I know that I have to be able to act on the spot, at the drop of a hat to get anywhere in my profession, but *I need time!*" When Lisa got up in front of the press conference, she was visibly shaking, and she "couldn't even hear half the press questions." All she could think was, "I look like a failure."

What is your impression of Lisa? Do you like her? How typical or atypical are her life experiences and her current behavior?

Does she need psychotherapy?

What do you believe are the core issues for Lisa? What is the utility of these initial formulations?

What overall goals for therapy do you suggest?

Before you read the next section, what topics and issues do you think will be addressed in the initial sessions?

Process Notes From Initial Sessions

When Lisa telephoned, I spent a few minutes discussing her situation and answering questions. I worked to get a sense of her difficulties before scheduling an initial session, in order to be certain that she was presenting problems within my expertise and to try to prevent emergency situations. I described the initial interview as a session in which Lisa would present her difficulties and I would offer an assessment and some treatment recommendations.

Most patients introduce themselves with their first name, and when, in the initial interview, I use the patient's first name, I take that opportunity to say, "I'm calling you 'Lisa.' Do you feel comfortable with that, or would you rather I called you 'Ms. Jones?'" Most patients prefer to be called by their first name. Then I say, "Since I'm calling you Lisa, you should feel free to call me 'Jackie.'"

I began the initial session by introducing myself and making a bit of small talk, "Did you find your way all right?" I began the formal part of the session by reiterating the agenda set in the telephone call, saying, "Our plan for today is to review your situation and to see what ideas I might have for you about treatment." I structured the session so as to obtain an overview of the patient's difficulties.

After this, I explained that Lisa seemed to have a social phobia and provided some information about this problem and its treatment options. I reviewed all available treatment options, including pharmacotherapy. I also offer a brief description of the approach I would take to this problem. In the case of Lisa's anxiety and social phobia, I stressed the key role of exposure in the cognitive–behavioral approach, as well as the need to learn new coping strategies and the importance of homework to the success of the therapy.

At this point, the ball was "in the patient's court" to make a decision about whether she wanted to work with me and try the CBT. Lisa made this decision easily and agreed to complete a homework assignment of reading the first chapter or two of a new popular book about social phobia, *Dying of Embarrassment*, before the next therapy session.

I ended the initial session with an invitation to Lisa to ask any questions she might have about me or my training or the treatment. The session ended with a discussion of money. I stated my fee and said, "I like to ask my people to write me a check at the time of the session. If you have any insurance reimbursement, of course I'd be happy to fill out any form your insurance company would like me to complete, but I would like to ask you to pay me, and then to seek reimbursement from your insurance company. If you have a use for it, I will send you a statement at the end of the month."

I began the second session by saying, "I would like to hear about how your week went and how the homework went. Also, at some point, today or next time, I'd like to get a sense of your background. Why don't we start with a review of the week and the homework, and then decide whether to take on some current business or do the history."

Lisa reported that she had completed the homework assignment and stated in general terms that she had found the book helpful. She had no pressing current business, so part of the session was spent collecting a personal, medical, and psychiatric history.

In the last part of the session, Lisa and I worked on a Thought Record, in which Lisa listed the typical automatic thoughts she experienced in speaking situations, such as "I'll make a mistake" and "Others will be critical and have negative views of me." I showed Lisa how these cognitions cause anxiety and suggested that relaxation strategies might be helpful. As homework, I suggested that Lisa begin working on relaxation strategies and continue to read the book.

I began the third session by asking Lisa how her week went, how her homework went, and what her agenda for the session was. Lisa reported that she had listened to the tape and done some more reading; she had no agenda for the session. Lisa reported that she had not had much anxiety because she had been avoiding speaking situations whenever possible. I focused again on the importance of exposure, and Lisa agreed that she would need to begin approaching feared situations and not avoid them. To begin this process, I suggested that a hierarchy of feared speaking situations be developed, and Lisa agreed. As a homework assignment, Lisa agreed to tackle one of the lower items on the hierarchy, rated as "20" on her scale, which was to chat informally with colleagues before each regular business meeting during the week, speaking for at least two minutes each time.

Were the initial sessions as you expected?

As you read this summary of the preceding sessions, are there any areas or topics that you think should be covered but were not? What other information would you seek to assess Lisa?

Before you view the tape, what do you think will unfold in the taped session? What issues will be discussed? What will the relationship between Dr. Persons and Lisa be like?

Viewer's Notes (Space provided for your notes.)

Stimulus Questions About the Videotaped Session

Dr. Persons begins the session by requesting a review of Lisa's week, an update on the homework assignment, and an agenda for this session. This structured opening is consistent with Dr. Persons' cognitive–behavior approach.

What responses and expectations does this type of opening evoke from the client? What do you think about this opening?

Lisa relates in detail her experiences with the homework assignments of approaching co-workers.

What are some reasons for and against behavior-by-behavior recount of homework assignments? Does performing these assignments help Lisa in resolving her presenting concerns?

In time-effective therapy, there are invariably choice points about what to discuss and what not to discuss. When reporting the fifth experience with the homework assignment, Lisa described the most awkward situation of the week. Lisa and Dr. Persons implicitly agreed that it was a different potential problem, and they chose not to address it at this time, in part because it raised conflicts beyond the immediate homework assignment.

Ideally, who, and on what basis, decides to shift or not shift the focus?

In identifying and listing ways of grappling with anxiety, neither Lisa nor Dr. Persons mentions the possibility of adjudicative use of antianxiety medication. Dr. Persons recommends exposure and response prevention in battling anxiety. Other mental health professionals might recommend short-term use of medication in this situation.

What would be your position in this specific situation?

Lisa proposed an unrealistic and expansive solution. The therapist immediately perceived the potential difficulties in this solution and suggested a more manageable tack.

What might have transpired in the session had Dr. Persons not identified the difficulties? Under what conditions might you have per-

mitted a patient to continue? How did Dr. Persons' redirection avoid Lisa's feeling criticized?

About 30 minutes into the session: Dr. Persons asks, "So how come it is taking me to help you figure this out?" This question could be interpreted by Lisa as an affirmation of her strength, as a criticism of her dependency or a misuse of therapy time, or as a paradoxical statement combining both elements.

How does the context and Dr. Persons' delivery influence Lisa's interpretation of the question?

In wrapping up the session, Dr. Persons suggests that Lisa write down her homework assignments and coping strategies. She later reminds Lisa to write these down when Lisa is not doing so.

What are some indications and counterindications of this procedure?

Dr. Persons takes notes throughout the session and in plain view of Lisa. Most therapists make notes on therapy sessions, but at different times and in different ways.

What do you do? What factors influence your decision about when and how you take your notes?

The session strikes many viewers as hopeful and encouraging.

What technical procedures or therapist behaviors contribute to this overall impression?

General Questions

Did the session progress as you anticipated? Was Lisa as you expected? Was Dr. Persons as you expected?

What are your general reactions to the session? What did you feel was effective in the therapy? What do you think were the strengths and the weaknesses of this approach?

If you were not informed that this is cognitive–behavior therapy, what would you have called it? What do you think makes this distinctly cognitive–behavior?

After reading about Lisa and viewing this session, what are your diagnostic impressions or characterizations of her problem?

How would you proceed with Lisa's therapy? How many sessions will it take?

Therapist's Reflections on the Demonstration

Dr. Persons, could you tell us a little bit about your reactions to this demonstration?

On the whole, I felt fairly positive about it. The strengths of the session were that I felt it was a good illustration of the collaboration, which I'm really working hard to get—the patient and I working together toward a common goal. The ideas I suggest seem reasonable to her. I'm always trying to check that out and be careful about that, not move too fast, and I felt that went well.

In what way was this demonstration typical or representative of your work, and in what way was it different?

It's typical in being a very task-oriented, problem-solving approach. We're working to identify the problem and generate some strategies for solving it. It's focused on concrete "here and now" problematic situations that the patient brings to the therapy as opposed to working on the early origins of problems.

It's very behavioral. I'm really focusing on a behavioral model, having a behavioral conceptualization. I'm working from the exposure model. Can we develop a hierarchy, and is the patient willing to work with me on starting at the bottom and working up through the stages of the hierarchy?

I'm also working on the collaboration. Homework is the key part of the model. So, all these are basic cognitive behavioral type of strategies.

In the session, we saw you come to agreement with the patient about her homework assignment for the next week. Would there be things that you would be thinking about between sessions? Would you have any homework for yourself?

The work we do is very detail-oriented—read a certain book, go to a certain room, go to a certain place. At the same time, I'm trying to keep in mind the larger picture. For example, this patient presents her central problem, the one she wants to work on, as this anxiety at work, such as difficulty coping in these speaking situations. She might have a social phobia, in general. I'm assuming that she has core beliefs such as, "I'm not really good enough when I'm in a demanding situation; I'm not going to be able to cope. I'm going to embarrass and humiliate myself. Other people are going to be critical and look down on me when I make a mistake." My task is to keep the overall picture in mind while guiding the focused work that we're doing at the moment.

Suggested Readings

Beck, A. T., Freeman, A., & Associates. (1990). *Cognitive therapy of personality disorders.* New York: Guilford Press.

Beck, A. T., Rush, A. J., Shaw, B. F., Emery, G. (1979). *Cognitive therapy of depression.* New York: Guilford Press.

Burns, D. D. (1989). *The feeling good handbook: Using the new mood therapy in everyday life.* New York: William Morrow.

Freeman, A., & Dattillo, F. (Eds.). (1992). *Casebook of cognitive–behavior therapy.* New York: Plenum.

Freeman, A., Pretzer, J., Fleming, B., & Simon, K. M. (1990). *Clinical applications of cognitive therapy.* New York: Plenum.

Kuehlwein, K. T., & Rosen, H. (Eds.). (1993). *Cognitive therapy in action: Evolving innovative practice* (pp. 33–53). San Francisco: Jossey-Bass.

Linehan, M. M. (1993). *Cognitive–behavioral treatment of borderline personality disorder.* New York: Guilford Press.

Persons, J. B. (1989). *Cognitive therapy in practice: A case formulation approach.* New York: Norton.

CHAPTER 12

Client-Centered Therapy

Conducted by Nathaniel J. Raskin, PhD

About Dr. Raskin

Nathaniel J. Raskin, PhD, was born in New York City in 1921. He graduated from the College of the City of New York (CCNY) in 1940 and received an MA from Ohio State University in 1941 and a PhD from the University of Chicago in 1949. He studied with Carl Rogers at both Ohio State and the University of Chicago. Currently, Dr. Raskin is Professor Emeritus of Psychiatry and Behavioral Sciences at Northwestern University Medical School, where he taught and did research in a clinical psychology program for 34 years. Since 1980, he has taught in person-centered learning programs in Italy, France, Switzerland, England, Slovakia, and Hungary and has spoken by invitation in Rome, Amsterdam, Cork, Moscow, and St. Petersburg. He continues a part-time private psychotherapy practice that began in 1950. Raskin is a Diplomate in Clinical Psychology, an APA Fellow, a Distinguished Alumnus in Psychology from CCNY, and was president of the American Academy of Psychotherapists from 1978 to 1980.

What do you know about Dr. Raskin? What are your impressions of his work from published material, conversations with and about him, or any other sources of information?

What are your expectations of Dr. Raskin's style and behavior in conducting psychotherapy?

Synopsis of Client-Centered Therapy

Provided by Nathaniel J. Raskin, PhD

As a client-centered therapist, I try to convey to my client implicitly, and occasionally explicitly, this cluster of attitudes: "I believe I can be of most help to you by offering you a relationship in which I try to understand, in your own terms, your problems, your feelings, your hopes and fears, the way you see yourself and others. As we go along, you will be able to correct me when my effort to understand is off the mark. Working with you in this way, I hope to help you clarify the problems that brought you here and how you might resolve them, to come to know yourself more fully, to like yourself more, and to become more of the person you want to be. I see myself more as a companion in this search than the traditional expert who figures out what is wrong with you. I will try, in our relationship, to understand the way you see and feel about yourself, your world, and others you choose to talk about, and to be a real person who respects your values and choices, even though they may be different from mine. I'll look to you to bring up whatever you choose in each session, to explore this or any other subject in your own way, to decide how often you would like to meet, and when you would like to stop coming."

Client-centered therapy was put forward by Carl Rogers in 1940 as an alternative to the existing orientations, which relied on guidance or interpretation. With his students at Ohio State University and then the University of Chicago, he carried out the first systematic and comprehensive research projects on therapy process and outcome. Using electronically recorded cases, evidence was provided that an orderly process of client self-discovery and actualization occurred in response to the provision by the therapist of a consistent empathic understanding of the client's frame of reference, based on an attitude of acceptance and respect. In 1946, the year that Carl Rogers was president of the APA, Rogers gave eloquent expression to the philosophy behind this approach:

"The client-centered therapist . . . has learned that the constructive forces in the individual can be trusted and that the more deeply they can be relied upon, the more deeply they are released. He has come to build his procedures upon these hypotheses, which are rapidly becoming established as facts: that the client knows the areas of concern which he is ready to explore; that the client is the best judge (of) frequency of interviews; that the client can lead the way more efficiently than the therapist into deeper concerns; that the client will protect himself from panic by ceasing to explore an area which is becoming too painful; that the client can and will uncover all the repressed elements which it is necessary to uncover in order to build a more comfortable adjustment; that the client can achieve for himself far truer and more sensitive and more accurate insights than can possibly be given to him; that the client is capable of translating those insights into constructive behavior which weighs his own needs and desires realistically against the demands of society; that the client knows when therapy is completed and he is ready to cope with life independently. Only one condition is necessary for all these forces to be released, and that is the proper psychological atmosphere between client and therapist."

Eleven years later, in 1957, Rogers defined this atmosphere in terms of a triad of "necessary and sufficient conditions:" empathy, congruence, and unconditional positive regard. This formulation stimulated a considerable body of research, providing substantial evidence of a correlation between these therapist-offered conditions and positive therapeutic outcomes, which client-centered theory defined in terms such as the expansion of self-awareness, the enhancement of self-esteem, a greater reliance on self for one's values and standards, and a more free, spontaneous, and open mode of experiencing oneself and the world.

Dr. Raskin identifies his approach as "client-centered therapy." What does this imply to you? More specifically, what do you expect of him? Will Dr. Raskin be active or passive? Will the session be structured or unstructured? Directive or nondirective? Will it focus on the past or on the present? Will the session focus on behaviors, on thoughts, or on feelings? What do you expect to be the relative balance between attention to technique versus the interpersonal interaction?

Have you, or has anyone you know, undergone client-centered therapy? What was it like? Was it helpful?

Client Background and Precipitating Events

Cynthia

Age: 30
Sex: Female
Race: African American
Marital status: Single
Education: BA
Occupation: Insurance representative
Parents: Father (50, regional sales manager); mother (49, office manager).
Siblings: One younger brother and one younger sister.
Grandparents: All deceased.

The parents have been married for 31 years. According to Cynthia, they have a good marriage. Her father is very respectful of her mother; in fact, he seems almost afraid of her. The father looks to the mother to handle all financial affairs and all business-related matters in the home. The father always supports the mother's behavior and her decisions. Of the two parents, her mother was the stronger disciplinarian, although both parents subscribed to the "spare the rod, spoil the child" model of child rearing. Both the mother and the father took out a lot of their verbal and physical frustrations on the children, especially Cynthia.

Despite her mother's harsh treatment her whole life, Cynthia loves her mother and treasures any kindness and affection from her. Her father has always seemed remote to her.

As a child and now as an adult, Cynthia received most of her love, attention, and affection from her brother and sister, who adore her, and she adores them. Although her parents seemed to take it easier on the brother and sister when they were growing up, Cynthia does not begrudge them their easier time. Cynthia feels that as the oldest it was her "place" to "take most of the licks."

Cynthia reports that as a child she was very nervous and a bed wetter.

Last weekend, Cynthia's boyfriend, Ken, invited some of his friends over to their apartment to watch a ball game. After the game, Ken and his friends were talking about politics, and although

Cynthia was not really involved in the discussion, she was listening and occasionally making comments. At one point, Ken said something that was "really out of line," according to Cynthia, and she contradicted his point. Ken continued to argue his point, and Cynthia added another comment. At this point, Ken got really loud, and yelled at her, "Shut up, fool, you don't know what the hell you're talking about." Cynthia left the room and went into the bedroom. She was hurt and angry, but she felt that it was best to button her lip until his friends left. Maybe he was right, she thought, even though she was upset with him. She figured that she could talk with him after his friends left.

When Ken's friends left, Cynthia went out into the living room to talk to Ken. She wanted to ask him how he could embarrass her so much in front of people, but before she could say a word, he started screaming and accusing her of embarrassing him in front of his friends. Cynthia was so angry at Ken for his reaction that she threw the glass she had in her hand at the wall and the glass shattered. Ken responded by slapping her on the face, telling her she was "unpredictable" and "out of control." Now furious, Cynthia lunged at Ken, and hit him. After that, Ken slugged her, and he knocked her to the ground.

Hurt, angry, and crying, Cynthia wondered, "What's wrong with me? Am I to blame? Is he right? Maybe I need help?"

In thinking through this event, Cynthia recalled that she had been in situations like this before. Two or three of her previous boyfriends had been abusive to her. She recalled one who seemed very sweet—almost like a "puppy dog"—but he would get very angry with her, and he would scream at her and call her an idiot. Another boyfriend actually got physically violent; he beat her around a few times, but she stayed with him for about 2 years. After these events, Cynthia was always left wondering if she was to blame. She asked herself, "Why am I drawn to these men? Why do I cause these things to happen? Is it all my fault?"

What is your impression of Cynthia? Do you like her? How typical or atypical are her life experiences and her current behavior?

Does she need psychotherapy?

What do you believe are the core issues for Cynthia? What is the utility of these initial formulations?

What overall goals for therapy do you suggest?

Before you read the next section, what topics and issues do you think will be addressed in the initial sessions?

Process Notes From Initial Sessions

Cynthia had telephoned and left a message on my answering machine that she was interested in an appointment. I returned her call as soon as I was able, recognizing that this kind of contact is usually not easy to make and that it was important to her to hear from me. On the phone as in person, I believe it is crucial to be sensitive to the client's expectations and feelings and to convey my interest and understanding. In this case when I returned her call, Cynthia, sounding upset, said that she had been in a recent fight with her boyfriend, that she did not know who was to blame, and that she thought she might need help because this kind of problem had occurred in earlier relationships. I listened and when she seemed to be finished, I tried to show my recognition of her distress, confusion, and feeling that she might be partially responsible. She indicated that she felt understood, and we arranged a mutually convenient appointment time. I ascertained that she knew where my office was and how to get there. She did not bring up the question of fees or insurance and neither did I, nor did I ask for any other information. I put a premium on what the client wishes to tell me and how. This is consistent with my belief that the client knows how far and fast she wishes to go, and that she is the best resource for problem identification, insights, and solutions.

In the first session, I sat down with Cynthia and waited for her to begin. I wished to convey to her, through my behavior rather than words of explanation and structuring, that this was a process that she was directing. She had myriad choices: She could launch right into her problem, tell me about her family, just sit and think for a while about what she wished to say, or ask about my way of working. From the very beginning, I looked to her to decide. If she had been uncertain, I would have articulated my understanding and acceptance of this feeling and given her a chance to explore it. In this way, the therapeutic process was set in motion at the outset, with my serving as a facilitator of my client's capacity to change, adapt, and grow. She was the driver, and I did not wish to delay her journey or interrupt her initiative by having her answer my questions, fill out forms, or complete a case history. In this instance, Cynthia began by talking about her boyfriend's unexpected outburst at her. The following is an excerpt from the interview:

Cynthia: It started with this ball game. Ken invited some of his friends over to watch the Redskins play the Giants. After the game, they got into a political discussion. I was mostly listening and not saying much. (Dr. Raskin: M-hm.) I didn't want to dominate things, but I thought I would be a better hostess if I offered an opinion. To my surprise, Ken got angry, and things started getting out of hand. So I left and went into the bedroom.

Dr. Raskin: You decided to leave the room when tempers started flaring.

Cynthia: Yes, I'd been putting so much into being a good hostess, I didn't want to spoil everything by getting into a fight.

Dr. Raskin: I see. A nice afternoon was suddenly turning into a disaster, and you thought the best thing you could do was to remove yourself.

Cynthia: Yes, I certainly wasn't expecting a fight, but if we were going to have one, I certainly didn't want it to happen in front of his friends. After they left, we did get into a fight. Ken turned on me and yelled that I had embarrassed him. I thought he had no right to scream at me, and I did something terrible; I threw my wine glass at him. It hit the wall and shattered.

Dr. Raskin: He made you furious, but you're ashamed of how you reacted?

Cynthia: Yes, it's not like me to do that, and I think people should talk things out when they get angry. Besides, it might have been my fault.

Dr. Raskin: You think maybe you're to blame for things getting out of hand between you.

Cynthia: Yes.

Cynthia then went on to recall incidents of being abused by the two men with whom she had been in relationships before Ken. She wondered if she had been to blame for those earlier situations. "Do I bring out the worst in these people?" She added, "I've also asked myself if I'm attracted to men like that?"

The first interview ended with my empathizing with her questions, "You've wondered if there's a pattern of your being drawn to men who are abusive and if you somehow stimulate that kind of behavior" and with Cynthia quietly assenting. She asked if she could see me again, inquired about my fee, and asked if she could use her insurance plan. I said that I could accept her insurance, told her my usual fee, ascertaining that this was acceptable to her.

If Cynthia had not brought up the question of fees, I probably would not have, either. I do not want to convey that "I want to make sure you can pay." This is not my attitude or my policy. In my experience, clients are almost always responsible in this area, and it is more important to me that I provide the service than that all my clients meet a set fee. Different clients can afford different amounts; my fee policy is flexible, and one aspect of my client-centered approach is to have the client involved in fee setting. Occasionally, I have been "burned," but I have chosen to pay this small price and make the business aspect of my practice secondary.

I deal with other issues, such as the client's telephoning me between sessions, as they emerge, rather than presenting a list of rules. I freely give my clients my home phone number and have not had reason to change this policy. If it is mutually convenient, I sometimes see clients at home. If my client is using a prescribed medication, I let him or her work that out with the prescribing physician and deal only with attitudes that may arise from this activity, such as fear of weight gain or a concern about excessive fatigue.

These policies and practices stem from a basic attitude of trust. I have a central and consistent interest and focus on my client's world of experience, within the context of a person-to-person relationship. I am willing to be seen in my home and to be known personally while not making myself the center of our interaction. In this area, too, my experience is that my openness has contributed warmth to the relationship without my being abused.

I have no typical second session. With Cynthia, I looked to her to bring up whatever was on her mind. I kept in mind what she had